Heart Room
and
Hyacinths

A wordsmith's journal of joy

DORI JEANINE SOMERS

iUniverse, Inc.
Bloomington

Heart Room and Hyacinths
A wordsmith's journal of joy

iUniverse books may be ordered through booksellers or by contacting:

iUniverse
1663 Liberty Drive
Bloomington, IN 47403
www.iuniverse.com
1-800-Authors (1-800-288-4677)

ISBN: 978-1-4697-7367-4 (sc)
ISBN: 978-1-4697-7368-1 (e)
ISBN: 978-1-4697-7369-8 (dj)

Printed in the United States of America

iUniverse rev. date: 2/17/2012

Where there's heart room, there's house room.

Norwegian proverb
Hvor det er hjerte rom, det huset rom.

If thou of fortune be bereft
And in thy store there be but left
Two loaves, sell one and with the dole
Buy hyacinths to feed thy soul.

from:
Not by Bread Alone
James Terry White
1907

Dedication

To all my beloved companions along the
way—parents, children, colleagues and friends—who
cared enough to request, remind, urge, nag, scold,
entreat, and encourage me
to write!

Table of Contents

WELCOME
where there's heart room
there's house room

We frail funny human beings live in story as fish live in water, and I am a storyteller. Writing has been at the center of my life, my skill and the gift of my spirit since I first became literate, so who better to tell this tale of feeding the soul? My story—an epic poem set in a world of change—is one my daughters and son have asked me to set down for them and for you. Write your story, our story, they said. Share what you have learned.

None of the things I've learned is new or startling. They inhabit what I have called the truth I knew, but didn't know I knew, until I gave it form upon a page. These discoveries might be the same for you—something you have held in your heart, even when your mind didn't note it.

I read somewhere that we'll never truly know what it's like in outer space, because we don't send poets there. So, listen with your heart to this poet's phrasing of some old and well-worn truths as they have appeared in my day-to-day living. You may recognize your own ideas spoken in a new way. Ralph Waldo

Emerson urged us to honor our own ideas, and I applaud his urging. Consider, if you will, that the thoughts that follow are simple reminders of your own inner wisdom, glimmers of your own special light. Dive into that pool of light, warm yourself in the pages before you, and make any words that brighten your day a part of your own inner glow.

Chapter one
Playing house and fording streams

Three years old.

Do I remember this, or simply the telling of it through the years? I was three years old when Duke, my German shepherd puppy, came to live with me. Our home was one of two citified two-story white houses on Orchard Avenue across from the golf course, at the edge of Merchantville, New Jersey. The family next door were the Brickleys.

My twelve-year-old sister June became friends with Jack, one of the Brickley boys, and on cold winter afternoons held me up to the kitchen window while Jack held up his little brother, Elwood, who was a toddler like me. I grew up saying Elwood Brickley was my first boyfriend, and we were friends for years, but we weren't neighbors for long.

My mother and father, Lil and Charlie Isaksen, whom I called Muz and Daddie, were brilliant at what today is called "flipping" a property—buying a fixer-upper and making it beautiful, then re-selling it. Before I turned four, Duke and the family and I moved to a cottage-style house in the woods of Delaware Township, and Daddie started his remodeling magic.

There was a huge ancient silver beech tree beside the house, two holly trees at the front door and a small forest behind the garage. Maple Avenue, the gravel road into the property, ended at our drive. There a farm field began, bordered by a meadow full of violets and yellow-bells. Muz and Daddie named our home "Road's End".

ROAD'S END

Speaking of naming, I'm writing this more than half a century later than the events, people and places in the story, so in my lexicon some of the names have changed. I no longer think of my folks as Muz and Daddie (that's his personalized spelling) but as Meme and Papa, the names awarded them by their grandchildren. Naming the elders is a privilege accorded to the "grands" in our family and carried forth with love, so...

I will say Papa built me a playhouse, big enough for the adults to visit, with a picture window at the rear and tall narrow side windows on each end. The front door opened onto a cement stoop with my name imbedded in it, and a swing hung between two wild cherry trees beside my little mansion. Inside was a white bench with an ornamental metal back and wooden seat, along with the usual doll's crib and miniature table and chairs where I served make-believe tea from an exquisite china cocoa set my grandmother, Jetta Erickson, had given me.

A fishpond shaped like a figure eight was a "feature" Papa built in the side yard, and when I got older, I started learning to ice skate on that tiny surface. With no sidewalks, I never did learn to roller skate, but from tumbles and spills I got plenty of cinders stuck in skinned knees and elbows. A beautiful lilac bush grew at the corner of our property and a laurel bush up the hill. Both of these formed great little cozies in which I could play house, using more imagination than the formal playhouse required. I made and shared with playmates a third great pretend house under a weeping mulberry tree that spread like an umbrella in a neighbor's yard.

I was born in Omaha Nebraska, where my dad had been stranded and left jobless because of the take-over of Victor Talking Machine Company by Radio Corporation of America (RCA). The Great Depression sent our family on the road, heading home to Jersey in search of a better life. We were all piled into an ancient truck with my crib in the back, and somehow made it to Camden County before my first birthday. There were six of us in our family then, my parents, my sister and baby Dossie (me) plus my mother's brother Frank whom she and my dad had raised since he was five. Uncle Frank had fallen in love with and married a quiet mid-western girl, a nurse named Ethel—my beloved Auntie Etts.

Ethel worked as a private duty nurse, sitting up with her patient through the night, and keeping herself awake with handwork. She sewed beautifully, and loved making clothes for June and me. Frank and Ethel were never blessed with babies, so I was sort of their surrogate child. They bought land adjacent to Road's End and planned their future home with a room for me. Sadly that never came to be, as Auntie Etts died of an enlarged heart when I was in third grade. This was my first encounter with grief and loss. Unkie never remarried.

My mother's mother had died when Meme was a young girl, and she became a self-taught Lady with a capital "L". She was gifted at creating elegance with little or no money, and called this one of her talents— robbing Peter to pay Paul. It was how she'd make ends meet, and she always managed to provide us with a gracious home where everyone felt welcome. Papa's Norwegian motto became the family heraldry: "Where there's heart room there's house room".

One of their money-raising projects was making hand-dipped chocolates to sell. Papa would boil the sugar to make fondant, pour the syrup on a slab of cold marble and using a plasterer's spatula turn the stuff until it became white and creamy for the centers of beautiful candies. Meme and Auntie Etts formed the shapes and Meme coated them with bittersweet chocolate, tapping off the drippings on her marble workspace until it made a glorious little mound beside the dipping pool. I see it still in my mind's eye, the design so elegant and rich. Easter eggs of various sizes sprouted names and flowers in colored sugar and egg white, and Christmas candies blossomed in fancy boxes. June, now in high school, found candy customers at Rice and Holman, the Ford dealership, and at the police station. Officer Rome Tull, the most handsome of cops, and Chief Linderman of the walrus mustache were among our favorites. Even today I can recall the smell of the Merchantville Police Station, redolent of cigars long past.

Papa was born in Brooklyn on February 29 in the year 1896. He had been promised that his mother would celebrate his birthday with a party when he was eight years old and the date actually occurred on the calendar, but his father died when he was seven, and his day was never celebrated. Not until he married his "Babe". Meme and his daughters always celebrated Papa's birthday every year, but with extra enthusiasm on those years that had 29 days in February!

Papa was an ardent labor union man, serving as shop steward for his fellow workers, who called him "Ike". His longtime connection to RCA Victor as a factory-based repairman brought with it popular music. He set up a record player in our living room with a microphone and leads to speakers throughout the house, and he hosted the teens' parties with dance-ability before anyone ever heard the term "disc jockey". We always had the latest hits.

My father was the hero of one family story, all about how easy-going and even-tempered he was—until he was pushed too far. From this particular story I learned that gentleness, patience, and forbearance can really be the hallmarks of power. We told the tale around our family's table of Papa's reaction to an unjust, unreasonable dictum when he was a young newlywed. In 1920 Lil and Charlie, like many young couples in the nineteen sixties and seventies, built a little house with their own hands, with Charlie creating kitchen cabinets, and Lillian up on the roof, hammering shingles. They filled in the marshy places on their land, and re-routed the drainage waters from the new highway into the recently cut town street in front of their little bungalow. With the pure drinkable water of an ancient Indian spring they had made a small pond in their private Eden. At this point the borough road department decided to flow the drainage back across their land in such a way that the pond would be polluted. Charlie's wise solution was to send the drainage flow underground by pipe, but—well, here is the poem that tells the story.

Gentle Strength
Among my family myths here is the finest that I know:
When Dad was young, he and my mother made a garden
    grow
Where brackish waters from the highway he'd drained to the
    street.
They built a cottage and a pond with waters pure and sweet.
He smiled his sunshine-lovely smile when answering the
    door,
And welcomed the official who had come to say, "No more
May you re-route the waters from the highway over there
Into the street. "Quite right", said Papa, "It seems very clear
The thing to do is pipe the water underground". "Oh, no!"
Officialdom insisted that the drainage had to go
Above the surface of his land— some silly useless rule
Or policy, unjust, inflexible— it meant the pool
Would be polluted needlessly. And Papa, so they say
Was moved by righteous anger. He was moved by rage that
    day
To dig his trench across his land, set pipe, refill and grade
In just a single afternoon. His protest thus he made.
Now, like my Papa, I have grown forbearing, patient, too...
Knowing the power of gentle strength that my father knew.

Oh, how I loved to read! When outdoors, I would sit in my swing or the hammock or sometimes up in a tree and

I'd snuggle in a big chair or on my bed when the weather changed. One of my early favorite childhood treasures was the beautifully illustrated *Adventures of Peterkin Pumperkin* in brown leather binding with gold letters.

Soon I discovered the works of Louisa May Alcott— *Little Women, Jo's boys, Eight Cousins, Under the Lilacs, Rose in Bloom*. Next came the works of Marguerite DeAngeli and then The Boxcar Children. Sister June taught me poetry. "Somebody's Mother", an old Victorian potboiler was about kindness. And Kipling's "L'Envoi" urges us to create for the love of the work and to paint the scene as we see it "for the God of things as they are". Both helped shape my values and my philosophy.

In our kitchen, there was always a comfortable-sized blackboard and plenty of chalk. Here messages could be found. If my mother needed to leave a note for us, she scrawled it on that blackboard, and we did the same. This was a good way to keep track of everyone, and I used it in my own home for years. I seem to recall a cat's sleeping place beneath my mother's venerable board, reserved for a huge white Persian named Mommy Cat. Duke never seemed to object to her being there.

From my bedroom window at Road's End, I looked out across acres of grain—oats, or soybean, mostly—to a farmhouse and barn on a slight rise more than a mile away. The field was cut in two by a creek that disappeared into the forest backing our land and ending at Highway 38, half a mile south. There were Indian arrowheads to be found in the creek, left by the Lenni Lenape. There were bridges to be built with fallen branches, and if you knew where to look, a clear pure spring bubbling in the woods. That spring was a lifesaver when summers were parched and our shallow well ran dry. When the grain in the field was fully grown I sometimes wove a small patch of it into a kind of mat, where I liked to lie and watch the pictures in the clouds. When there was snow, Duke and I made magical pathways through the fields.

My large collection of dolls took up most of my bed and filled a few built-in storage drawers. Every Christmas Auntie Etts made gorgeous new outfits for them, especially the Dossie doll which was a Shirley Temple doll that my Norwegian Bestamor's (grandmother's) Swedish hubby, Alec Erickson, bought because he thought she looked like me. This jolly Swede called me Grumpa's Gurl and took me on walks for ice cream cones whenever we visited them in Keansburg on the Jersey shore. Keansburg, called "The Burg", was a ferry trip away from NYC and a two-hour drive from Road's End. How much I loved the family's singing as we traveled in the car, especially the old songs like "Side By Side" "Always" and "My Kid" that my parents sang. June and Papa sang at home while we did dishes together. On our way to Keansburg we eagerly watched for a tall smokestack marking the refuse incinerator on the edge of town that signaled our arrival at The Burg.

Papa's aunt, Tanta Serena, my grandmother Jetta's younger sister, was a rather fey old dear. She had lost her daughter to a childhood illness and with that tragedy lost her stability. Serena lived with my grandmother, and showed me how to put a nickel in the box that controlled the water heater. I also remember Tanta Leeva (Aunt Olivia) who was the matriarch of the Isaksen clan, with a house in The Burg where dozens of Norwegian-American cousins gathered. Papa's cousin Alice had a son Allan, my second cousin, who gave me my "first kiss" in a grape arbor, while we nestled on a glider swing. The fence behind my bestamor's house was covered in yellow honeysuckle, different from the wild pink blossoms in our woods at Road's End, but just as fragrant. Papa's cousin Edna (Aunt Edna to me) lived and worked in New York City where she bought her daughter (little Edna) stunningly stylish clothes. Little Edna was about two years older than I, and as she outgrew her wardrobe, Aunt Edna boxed the clothes up and sent them to me. The arrival of those packages was a merry little Christmas any time of year!

Road's End backed the side of a neighbor's property toward their back gate. They were the Preston family, Florence and Clifford and their sons, David, Leonard and Walter. June was best friends with the oldest son, Dave, who sang beautifully. There had not been a daughter born in the Preston family for several generations and even Mom-mom and Pop-pop, the Preston grandparents, were longing for a little girl. And here was I, a curly-headed blonde four-year-old with bright-eyed curiosity and a gregarious personality. Aunt Floss, as I was invited to call her, let me make Jello in her kitchen, and help her bake cakes, tickle the piano keys, and generally become an adopted family member. When Leonard and Walt's school, J. H. Coles, had its big annual festival (Field Day it was called) the Prestons invited me to attend with them. Meme dressed me in a lovely girly frock of blue dotted Swiss, and the boys, coming from a musical family, serenaded me with the old song, "Alice Blue Gown", making that beautiful dress my Alice blue gown forever after.

Another dress that brought me some attention was yellow with matching socks and a little yellow coat. Meme dressed me in this outfit and took me to the theatre to see the famous comedian and radio star, Joe Penner, known for his gag line: "Wanna buy a duck?" I rode on Papa's shoulders and when we visited backstage, the comedian called me his little canary and presented me with a china cream pitcher shaped like a duck. It sat in my mother's china closet for years.

In the fall after I turned five I started first grade at Coles School. Meme and Unkie took me on the first day, and stood around metaphorically wringing their hands while some youngsters cried and carried on about being left alone. I looked at those kids with disgust and told Meme and Uncle Frank it was time for them to leave. Peeking back through the window in the door, they watched as I comforted the one child whose tears I didn't disapprove—little Marjorie Haffrel, whose tears were OK because she was such a tiny one.

Just up the lane from Road's End were the girls I played with most often, Nancy Dreegar and her aunt (who was the same age as she) Betty McComb. We galloped about on long bamboo poles, pretending they were horses as we raced through a gravel pit, playing at being beautiful cowgirls, like Belle Star. We rode our bikes on the rough gravel of Maple Avenue, fell down and skinned our knees. No iodine, please!

The first Broadway show I ever saw was Winged Victory, which I attended with Meme, Papa and June when I was about eight years old. I was captivated from the first lifting of the curtain, and became a life-long theatre lover. Summers we usually spent Papa's two-week vacation at a rented cottage or apartment on the Jersey shore, and one year the four of us traveled to Montréal, Canada, did the regular tourist trek and laughed over the silly jokes we girls made up.

Family vacation time.

As a schoolgirl I did very well academically, but never athletically. This made me a target for a few of the school bullies, but that was less a part of my childhood than the safe and steady atmosphere where I could walk a mile alone along a country road, cross a major highway and take the bus into Merchantville for Girl Scout meetings where we made gollywog pins from halved corks, thumbtacks, and black wool pompoms. The bus stop across from the Merchantville town hall was guarded by Officer Tull and all was well. Rome Tull was not the only policeman in my story, however. There was Unkie, who became a Delaware Township constable, and made me very proud. Sometimes I was with him in the car when he went after speeders, and that was really exciting for a little girl. He seemed to know everybody. He joked with the famous heavyweight boxer, Jersey Joe Walcott, and was friends with him long before he fought Joe Louis for the championship.

At J. H. Coles School I started something new in seventh grade—a newsletter. I called it the JHC Comet, designed and drew the letterhead, with the "C" as the head of the comet. Little did I know how many more newsletters and news columns were to come in this long and literary life of mine! My eighth grade teacher somehow found a source of funding for library books, and I was one of the elite few chosen to shop for them. This entailed a trip to Philadelphia. We took a bus to Camden and went by ferry across the Delaware River to Philly. Then up Market Street to the city's wonderful storybook department stores—Lit Brothers, Strawbridge and Clothier, and of course, John Wanamaker. The Wanamaker store was a wonderland with its huge central open gallery so many stories high, its magnificent pipe organ peeling out songs from the mezzanine, and on the main floor the great bronze sculpture of the American Eagle! In Philadelphia you usually made your arrangements to get together with a friend saying, "Meet me at the Eagle".

I have no idea how they came to be friends, but my Papa, who left formal education at about eighth grade, had a long and treasured friendship with Dr. Guy Cameron, a professor at Princeton University. I recall going with Papa on visits to Professor Cameron's home. His stately house was furnished in antiques and books, and those visits became an inspiration in my life. Surely I would grow up to study at Princeton! But Papa and the professor laughed when I declared my intent to study at our friend's college. I couldn't understand the men's laughter. How was I to know Princeton was then available only to male scholars? Alas! I was born too early to become a proper Princetonian!

When I was about twelve, Meme and June enrolled in a pottery class and began making lovely things, like candy dishes and ceramic lilies for lapel pins. This may have planted the seed that blossomed for June in her forties when she went back to college and became a ceramicist. Their work intrigued me so that I tried my hand at modeling clay, and made a little Buddha which has decorated my space in every home along my way, ever since. Eventually, I learned to treasure Buddha for more than his aesthetic glory.

My big sister was always surrounded by various beaus and admirers, like Dave Preston and a sweet young man from Haddonfield, named Winfield Kay. These two often joined our family on winter evenings, when we went ice-skating on one of the local lakes, then home again for cocoa and cake. Food was a major part of hospitality in those days, without thought of calories. My mother had a little epitaph she sometimes claimed as her own: When I die, let all men utter/ She was a cook who never skimped on butter!

Win Kay began taking June horseback riding, and generously took little sister along. I quickly learned to handle a horse and could hardly wait for our mornings at the riding academy. The owner of the academy dubbed me "Penny" as in lucky penny, because he said he sold horses more easily when prospective buyers saw how good the steeds looked with a little girl on mount.

When World War II began, Dave went into the Army, Win 'the Paratroopers, and my dear Unkie the Coast Guard. Everyone treasured letters from our boys in the service, and I was a faithful correspondent to all three. Knowing how much I loved riding, Win sent me money to finance a few rides while he was away, but this was wartime, so I chose to buy Victory stamps instead. He said he was proud of me.

When I graduated from eighth grade, the Isaksen family moved from Road's End into a large house on a lovely tree-lined street in the middle of Merchantville. I started high school, and learned to love Shakespeare, Browning and art class. Staying after school to work on my first oil painting (a reedy marshlands scene with mallards) I met a new friend, our high school janitor Mr. Jack Foster. He was a folksy poet who often stopped by the art room to admire the students' projects and chat a bit. His poetry appeared in the *Community News* from time to time and I especially loved his "Kickin' Through the Leaves", about the joy autumn brings throughout a lifetime. He was inspiration for a nascent poet unaware.

June graduated from Merchantville High School in 1939 and in the mid forties went on to West Jersey Hospital for training to become a Medical Technician. Her first medical job was at a little hospital in Riverside, where she lived in the nurses' dorm. Oh, how I missed her!

Although my folks were not churchgoers to any great degree, they had enrolled me as a child in the Sunday school of Trinity Methodist Church in Merchantville at the corner of Center Street and Chapel Avenue. Local stories told of a still that operated at the other end of the road during prohibition. That still for many years lent its persona to the name of the byway, called Whiskey Road. Then the beautiful little Trinity Church, with its stained glass windows and curved front steps was built and challenged the community ethic. Whiskey Road came to be called Chapel Avenue. As a preteen, I became a member of the Methodist Youth Fellowship (MYF) and joyfully attended Sunday evening potluck suppers every week, enjoying the lime jello salad and other comfort foods. I even sang in the youth choir. Singing at Trinity was special because one faithful member of the church was the tenor Eddie Roecker. This handsome actor played the role of the Red Shadow in Romberg's Desert Song—along with all the other operetta roles he sang so beautifully—more than any other actor in the country.

During the summer following my freshman year of high school, I went to MYF "camp" at Pennington, a prestigious prep school in Lawrenceville, near Princeton, NJ. Marjorie Haffrel, the little girl I'd met on my first day of school, went too. As we sat on the lawn on the first evening of our weeklong adventure, I saw a great looking fellow from one of the MYF chapters in South Jersey, and pointed him out to Margie. She was quite interested. Later that week, it turned out the young man, Oscar Carter Somers, was not interested in Marjorie, but in me. As we became friends, then boyfriend and girlfriend, I learned his family and close friends called him Buz. We kept in touch by mail, and Buz invited me to his band concert in Wenonah, and eventually to his first formal dance. My mother made my gown, and I stayed with the Somers family for the weekend. His parents, Oscar senior and Mildred (called Mid) were delighted that Buz had chosen a nice acceptable girlfriend.

Taffy and Buz ready for band concert.

After just a year in our Merchantville home, Meme and Papa found a buyer and announced we were moving, all the way to Mt. Holly (about fifteen miles away). Having just gotten used to my new school, I was devastated.

Chapter two
New girl in town

Mt. Holly - The good news was that June was working at Burlington County Memorial Hospital, so our move meant she could live at home. The house at 23 Buttonwood Street was an exquisite revolutionary era brick home with cedar floors and a small white front porch. It was just up the street from the Methodist Church, Friends Meeting and the downtown shops. Papa once again worked his magic to upgrade the kitchen, make a recreation room in the basement and with Meme's tasteful decorating, to create a masterpiece of elegance.

With Ralph, Meme, and June by Twenty-three Buttonwood Street.

June and I chose to share the top floor bedroom spanning the width of the house, with tall windows overlooking the mount on one end and Hack's Canoe Retreat on the other. It was a ballroom of a bedroom. No partitioning it into separate rooms for us!

In the spring, we girls were gifted with an Old Town canoe. I painted a blonde Indian maiden on one side of the prow, labeled her "Taffy", the name given me by my sister several years before, because of my Nordic locks. I painted a brunette named "June" on the other side and added the quirky boat's name we'd chosen: "Gotno Brave". Our little craft became a familiar sight along the cedar banks of the Rancocas River or in her birth at Hack's Canoe Retreat. Often one or the other of us shared our water travels with a person of the male persuasion but when someone pointed out an apparent discrepancy in the name "Gotno Brave", we'd insist the guy wasn't all that daring.

Sledding down the mount, past the cemetery and down Buttonwood Street was the big thrill of the winters, usually restricted to the young male population. But I couldn't resist such fun, and joined the daredevils on the hill whenever I could. On Christmas Eve the Isaksen house was a popular stop-off place for everyone, because we sisters were to be found playing popular records, decorating a tree and serving lots of festive foods. At Halloween or Fourth of July Mt. Holly held parades and a huge downtown block party with a bandstand and music for dancing. Before big football games there were pep rallies and bonfires the whole town came out to enjoy. My big surprise about the move to Mt. Holly was the happiness it brought me. As the new girl in town, I was somebody special. No longer identified as June's kid sister, as in Merchantville. I was "Taffy", a sophomore who was part of the senior clique, a party-giving maven and writer of a column in the local paper. In fact, June came to be known in Mt. Holly as Taffy's sister!

There were summer jobs to be sought when one was in high school, so I signed up for blueberry picking the summer after we made our home in Mt. Holly. Each morning a truck would pick up the young pickers on the main street of town, and take us to the fields of high-bush "True Blues" the size of grapes. We got unbelievably dirty from the black coating on the berries, and oh so tired, but we earned a few pennies for our summer expenses. My other jobs in those years included retail sales at the news shop, where I sold publications, greeting cards and roasted peanuts, witch I was charged with roasting, and hand painting ties and scarves to order, usually with portraits of beloved pets. I was particularly thankful for a family of boxer fanatics who had their champions immortalized by my brush and helped line my purse.

After football games or dances the favorite gathering places for Mt. Holly kids were "The Cup", on the edge of town, a funky cup-shaped ice cream shop and hamburger joint in the manner of the Brown Derby, or "Gardner's" in Moorestown, the next town west, where the high school was our biggest rival. Frank Gardner was a classmate of mine and his brother a Mt. Holly grad. The fact that their dad's eatery was in bad ole Moorestown always amused us, and the family restaurant appealed to us and our parents as well. One of Meme's little jokes was to sip her milkshake, and when the straw was about to make its hit-the-bottom noise, she'd say, "Everybody stamp your feet", so we couldn't hear her slurping the last of the shake.

When there were big dances at the high school, my sweet parents would cater a dinner party for my friends, and me complete with fine china, sterling and crystal, flowers and gourmet goodies. There were never any broken dishes or unseemly behaviors, and we young folks in our formal wear had the time of our lives.

Buz and I saw each other from time to time, he making the trip for my sweet sixteen party, and I attending occasional events at his school as well, but the distance limited visits between Wenonah and Mt. Holly.

Freshman year in Merchantville I had played field hockey and as a poor runner to begin with, I struggled in the position of left wing until I tore the cartilage in my right knee. In my elastic and steel brace there was to be no playing hockey in my sophomore year so I volunteered instead to manage the Mt. Holly team. I served them oranges and cool drinks after the games, which was fun, but it lasted only one year because the yearbook advisor decided to try something new. For the first time there would be a non-senior on the yearbook staff. She asked me to serve as assistant editor during my junior year, in preparation for being editor-in-chief of the forty-niner's book. Yearbook sessions were scheduled at the same time as hockey practice. My office was beside the exit to the girl's gym, and with mixed emotions, I watched "my team" coming and going to games or practice as I worked on write-ups, layouts, photos and artwork.

The business portion of the job involved negotiating and planning print runs with Cal Louderback our print manager, from the local weekly, the *Herald*, and at 16, I managed to win this professional's respect and admiration with my organization and writing skills. I'd been active in getting a teen center opened in town, and Cal introduced me to the editor of the *Herald* and convinced him I should write a column about Mt. Holly youth. The "Rec" as our YWCA-sponsored teen center was known, was the topic of my weekly column, and I spent Friday evenings dancing and gathering news bits while making even more friends.

One new friend was a tall dark and handsome farmer from Burlington, named Ralph Dyson, who played piano by ear and won my heart with his music. Ralph taught me to drive in his Ford pick-up, and romanced me when the fragrance of alfalfa filled the air. I didn't see him exclusively, but I sure loved his rendition of "Tea for Two"!

In addition to my writing and editing in Rancocas Valley Regional High School, I was known for acting in all the school productions and for being the only girl in the Stagecraft Club doing set decoration and design. *Our Hearts Were Young and Gay* was the senior play in which I had a supporting role, and another review type show put me in a large picture frame just off the proscenium, gowned in sparkling white, under an amber spot as I told the story of "Blue Roses". My sister liked the way I looked so much she threatened to follow me around with an amber spot!

June left Mt. Holly during my junior year to work at Walter Reed Army Medical Center in DC. She talked a lot about one of the young doctors, Arthur Dietrick, whom she called Bud. She said she thought he was just right for me, and wanted to get us together. He came to visit. At the end of the weekend, I took my sister aside and said, "This guy's in love with you. And you're in love with him. I know, because of the way you talk about him. Now either you have a relationship with him, or shut up. I don't want to hear about him again!" She was stunned. I'd never confronted her like that before. On the way back to Washington, he proposed and she accepted!

Which brings us to Christmas Eve, 1948, when June and I stood on a ladder to hang mistletoe in the foyer of number twenty-three, and to place our baubles on the tree. One of the locals who stopped by during the evening was a white-bearded fellow in a red Santa suit who brought us candy canes on his way to a Kiwanis party. Others included six (count 'em, six!) young men who glared at each other throughout the evening. Never mind the happy carols and the sweet smell of balsam. One of the fellows was Ralph Dyson who wanted to give me an engagement ring, and the others, various hopefuls who wanted me to say no. The stress of that evening persuaded me to abandon "playing the field" and settle down. Ralph and I even bought a piece of land near his family farm, and I designed a ranch house that we planned to build. We went to my senior prom together, but the engagement lasted only a few months after that. My dreams were all about college.

I was one of the three best-known artists in the high school art department, and wanted to make my career in art. The teacher told me, as the fifties loomed on the horizon, that women couldn't make it in the world of commercial art, so perhaps I should consider teaching. Somehow that suggestion never took root. My love of painting, however, knew no bounds. When I decided the week before a school dance that the clothes in my closet would easily provide an outfit for the event, my mother disagreed, offered me her Lit Brothers charge token, and sent me all the way to Philly to find a dress for the dance. I came home without the new dress, but with a lovely red sable watercolor brush, instead. Briefly I worked at a ceramic studio painting with "slip" on unfired pots. Then Meme and Papa found another house to remodel and they moved back to Delaware Township, (now called Cherry Hill) on the exit road from the Cherry Hill Race Track. This house they named "The Birches".

Chapter three
This filly loves Philly

I moved to The Birches with my folks, and began commuting to Philadelphia, working at the Provident Trust Company at the corner of Seventeenth and Chestnut Streets. It amused me to discover the bank had originally been founded to do business "with Quakers and persons of like conservative habits". Starting in the bookkeeping department, I learned how to use a dinosaur of a bookkeeping machine, which drove me to distraction with boredom. Eventually they moved me to the main floor as the first woman in the banking department. My desk sat beneath the great Millet painting, "The Gleaners" from which grand location I sent messengers out to collect on my customers' stocks and bonds, and used a special wireless code for the purchase of foreign monies. Evenings, I studied at the American Institute of Banking and earned a Primary certificate. I also attended classes at a Philadelphia modeling school, but I'm not sure why. I did learn how to walk gracefully and angle my body for snapshots, but to what end? I think this was part of the trend known as "charm school". Philadelphia was beautiful. I loved it all—walking on Chestnut Street, looking in the windows at Lane Bryant, meeting Eugene

Ormandy, conductor of the Philadelphia Orchestra, or Ernie Kovacs from WCAU, visiting art exhibits on Rittenhouse Square while sucking on a lemon-stick, (a porous-centered hard candy stuck into a fresh lemon) or buying picnic lunches in the Springtime to share with a friend in the pavilion behind the Philadelphia Museum of Art!

One afternoon I saw a familiar face on Walnut Street. It was Cal Louderback from the *Mt. Holly Herald,* now publisher of the *Philadelphia Chamber of Commerce News,* who had his office in a neighboring building. He offered me a job writing for the paper, and I couldn't wait to tell my parents when I got home. My mother, much to my amazement, said no. She was adamant, insisting I mustn't leave the bank because they had "invested in me". Like a good girl, I did as mother told me, and missed out on writing for what became *Greater Philadelphia Magazine.* Another Helen Gurley Brown nipped in the bud! During this time of my young adulthood, I sometimes suffered from what I called "stomach headaches" because the severity of the pain seemed to continue until I was sick to my stomach. This malady was undoubtedly psychosomatic. Although I was without the pressures of independent living, I felt instead the pressure of a need for freedom. I was trapped in an era when "good girls didn't…" You name it. We didn't do it. We certainly didn't strike out for ourselves and live alone, suffering parental disapproval.

I took advantage of the Philadelphia "First Nighters", program that made theatre tickets available at an affordable price, and saw Ann Bancroft in *Two for the Seesaw,* Bobby Morse in *How to Succeed in Business,* and other great shows in their pre-Broadway run at the Shubert. I took my dad to see Yves Montand in concert, and enjoyed Eugene Ormandy's

Philadelphia Symphony from high in the nosebleed seats at the Academy of Music. I sat there, too, with a Baptist student from Crozier Seminary, and discovered I wasn't ready for fundamentalist theology. Didn't date him for long!

While I was busy becoming a workingwoman, Buz Somers was off at Alleghany College in Meadville, PA. He regularly invited me to parties and dance weekends, which meant flying from Philadelphia to Pittsburg, and air travel was always elegant. Ladies wore hats and gloves, and looked like fashion models. Only those who traveled by bus would make a trip in their grubbies! Buz and I kept up a stream of letters throughout his college years—mine usually encouraging him and cheering him on like an advice column from "Old Auntie Dee". He played the sax and loved music, especially the LPs of Freddie Gardner, an alto sax man who died quite young. Because of our long distance friendship and romance, our song was "All the Things You Are" which begins: "You are the promised kiss of springtime that makes the lonely winter seem long..." Sweet! In the beginning, the boy danced "like a Methodist", but he soon improved. My Papa had danced with me in his arms before I could walk, and anyone who wanted to date me had better be ready to dance. Vacation time, when he was home from school, I visited the Somers family in Plainfield NJ or Buz visited at the Isaksen's, and we went dancing. That was the most romantic part of our time together—the dancing. We whirled about to the "good, good music of Oscar Dumont and his orchestra at Sunset Beach in Almonesson, New Jersey". We loved to dance!

Each year the Junior League of Mt. Holly put on their New Year's Eve Ball at the Armory, and the Isaksen family reserved a large table in the balcony. Papa and Unkie were there, and later Bud and Buz or whoever I was seeing—all so handsome in their tuxedos. And the ladies were beautiful and elegant in gowns and flowers. Oh, but my Papa and Unkie could dance! Doc and I would jive or jitterbug and call it the Lindy. When the Dietricks came home from Bud's time in the Air Force and settled in Mt. Holly another tradition was born—attending the Doctors' Dance. This was as elegant as the New Years Eve Ball, and served as a yearly gift or thank you to friends from Dr. Dietrick and Mrs. Doctor. They always gave a pre-dance party in their lovely home, featuring Old Fashioned Cocktails, Papa's Punch, and June's famous miniature (secret recipe) party meatballs.

One of the boys I dated while Buz was away at college was an NYU law student I met at the bank. Joe Restifo was bright and sophisticated, and very low key. I visited him in Greenwich Village one autumn and was surprised to see my photo on his bedroom wall. He took me to see Glass Menagerie by Tennessee Williams at the Circle in the Square, and caressed my shoulder as it peeked from my scoop-necked black dress. "If it's uncovered," he said, "it's going to get kissed". He brought me a Christmas present that year, a little gold watch. Once again my mother said "no". This was too grand a present for me to accept. Joe chuckled and said, "If I was all that serious it would have been a ring". Years later I had lunch with Attorney Restifo, and found he had become a stuffy old conservative. No loss there! Or perhaps he would have broadened his outlook had we remained close.

These were the years when I first discovered my Muse. Often in and out of love as a passionate young woman, and searching for myself and meanings for my life, I began to express myself on pads of paper and notebooks. To my amazement and delight, I found a kindred spirit on the bus to Philadelphia. Another young businesswoman and fellow poet waiting at my bus stop became my friend as we compared hearts and minds with words set to our own inner music. It saddens me to realize I don't even remember her name, yet we changed each other's lives with our poems.

Tommy, a musician who came into the bank one day, also connected on the level of spirit. I visited his bare center-city apartment and sat at his feet on the floor as he played his compositions on a piano that was the room's only furnishing. We ate brown bread and cheese with olives and grapes, simply enjoying the quiet together. The next day I received a note with a few lines of poetry from him, thanking me for bringing in spring with such gentle beauty. Shortly after our visit he left for Paris.

For a while I roomed with my cousin, Flo, and her very large husband, Ed Shabacker, in the Philadelphia suburb of Germantown. Ed had a quirky sense of humor and came up with wry comments and funny names for things. He was most thrifty and loved strange things like Limburger cheese. A memorable character, he. While staying with the Shabackers, I slept on a sofa in their sun-porch, showered in an industrial style shower stall in the basement, and traveled to work in center city on the subway and the el. At that time I was writing regularly to my high school classmate and friend, Jack McDonnel, who was studying to become a dentist. He phoned fairly often to chat with me, and so Ed began calling him "the foolish young man". The cost of long distance phone calls earned him this sobriquet.

While I was still a little girl my folks had introduced me to Chinese food at the Cathay Tea Garden in Philadelphia, and as I grew older we found new Chinese restaurants on our Friday evening family outings to Camden. Fridays included grocery shopping with Papa at the Giant Tiger market and clothes shopping with Meme and sister June at the Style Nook or Billie & Dave's Sportswear. Billie (the wife) and Dave were a stunning Jewish couple who became fond family friends, as did Miss "B" the manager of Style Nook and the owner's daughter. Miss "B" made regular seasonal buying trips to New York, and always brought back some fashions chosen with June, Meme or me in mind. The folks at the Style Nook treated us like royalty.

When Buz graduated from Alleghany College he was called into the Army, and chose to forgo a commission, which would keep him in the service for longer than the two years required by the draft. He entered the army as a private, and was stationed at Fort Dix in central Jersey. Buz renewed and intensified his courtship over the shorter distance and our song played in our heads… *someday I'll know that moment divine, when all the things you are, are mine.* I was actually considering marrying this young man who had been part of my life for seven years. In an attempt to use reverse psychology, Meme and Unkie acted disinterested in the Somers boy and his suit for my hand. (Maybe she'll rise to his defense if we pretend he's not much.) Well, I don't know if that plan worked or we just discovered, after all that long-distance dating, that we were in love and ready to make the big commitment, but we did get engaged.

I thought June weddings were much too common, and I never wanted to be a June Bride, but Uncle Sam had different plans.

Overseas orders came through for Private Somers and the wedding had to be in June or not until some two years hence. So off I went to the Style Nook for a conference with Miss "B". She went to New York and found a fairy princess wedding gown for me. It was made of white nylon lace designed with crowns and roses inspired by the 1953 coronation of Elizabeth II and billowed gracefully over a small hoop-skirted petticoat. My mother made a lace Juliet cap and off-the-face veil to complete my bridal elegance. I chose awareness over glamour by keeping my glasses firmly on my nose.

June 23rd we were wed at Trinity Church and honeymooned for three days in central Jersey. We made the mistake of seeing a three-D movie (bad stuff in those days!) and I got quite sick from it, (sort of like seasickness) but we had one day in New York City where we saw *Porgy and Bess*, on Broadway, which was stunning. Just for us...*Summertime! Somerstime?*

Buz shipped out for Germany in August, and for the first time I resisted my mother's nay saying. She objected to our plans for me to follow my husband to Germany and live "on the economy", as it was called, without government support. In February I sailed on Holland America's *SS Ryndam* for Rotterdam.

Chapter four
Abroad in the wider world

Off to Europe!

The mid-winter crossing was rough but exciting, with plenty of fascinating companions on board. There were ski-bums and returning diplomats, a student from *école des Beaux Arts* in Paris, a young female museum curator, a Pasteur Institute chemist and other cosmopolitan types. We drank Dutch beer, and named ourselves the Blotto Grotto, playing charades and "stink- pink", a rhyming game with adjective/noun combinations. For example, an untidy auto would be a sloppy jalopy. Crossing the Atlantic on a great ship is like leaving reality behind and entering a world unto itself for seven days, with lovely meals, new "best" friends, games and laughter. Because of her high outline the Ryndam reacted to the stormy seas of February by tossing us about enthusiastically. We affectionately dubbed her the Roll-damn. I went through two pairs of glasses, and acquired a few bruises, but never stopped enjoying the trip. The Dutch crew was delightful, and openly friendly to Americans, and our special waiter loved to show off his skill at peeling an orange in a single swipe.

Buz met me in Rotterdam and we traveled several hours by train to the little German town of Pirmasens, where he was stationed. He had rented a room for us in the home of Frau and Herr Pietch, and there we began our European adventure. His work kept Private Somers busy behind a desk at the US ARMY Signal Corps depot, and he had to get a pass each night in order to leave the base and come "home" to his wife. We were allowed some use of the Frau's kitchen, but mostly I cooked on a hot plate and kept our food on an outside windowsill. As an American living in Germany without dependent status, I couldn't use the P X, so I learned to shop at the local market. Buz had studied German in College, but I had to pick up the local patois on my own, and was thrilled when I could name the things I wanted to buy. Carrying my little string bag, I'd collect a few eggs, or some potatoes and a schnitzel or beefsteak, and marvel on the way home that I'd succeeded. Then I'd inwardly smile about the folks with fragrant sausages in their briefcases and the little guys who looked like spacemen riding by on their motorbikes.

There was a tiny pocket park just down the block from the Pietch house, with a statue in the center. Our "Saint George and The Dragon" sculpture inspired lots of photo opts for the Somers kids and other American tourist types. Each region has its own dialect—potatoes, for instance, are called *kartofflein* in formal Deutsch, but the local word was *grumpeelers*—and while struggling with my German I met and tried to talk with an elderly woman in the park. Hearing my version of her language, she decided I must be from some town across the mountain. I didn't tell her my mountain was the Atlantic Ocean and the town was America.

Newly-weds in Germany.

Our landlady, Frau Pietch was a *Damenschneiderin*, a women's dressmaker, and from time to time she would ask me to model a dress she was making for someone in the village. During the fittings she would fuss over the delicacy of my lingerie, exclaiming, "*Zu kaelte!*" Too cold! I think she expected me to bundle up in long johns. In the bathroom a boiler above the tub ground out hot water, but for a good shower or sitzbad (tub bath) a person needed to visit the town baths. The Stadtbad served as a social gathering place much like today's popular fitness centers. Our own little room became a social center, too, a veritable second home for two of Buz's Army buddies, and a place where we grew to be friends with Carol and Bob, the other American couple renting a room in the Pietch house.

On Buz's days off, our favorite pastime was castle hunting. With typical American fervor, we explored the burg and schloss ruins and reconstructions. Castles, after all, were something we didn't see at home. Sometimes our Army pals would come along, and always we brought the camera.

Once, when Buz was off duty, we visited Munich, where the Hoffbrau House served huge steins of hearty German beer and rosettes of sweet white Munchner radishes. We sang along with the crowd while standing on our chairs and waving our steins in the air and learned the words to the joyful songs. On a boat tour down the Rhine, we saw *die Lorelei* and more castles. In Heidelberg we visited the great Heidelberg Castle, and in the evening we sat in a gasthaus at a long table with university students and drank the delicate white wine called *liebfraumilch*. Once we even dined on wild boar. I'd expected it to taste like pork, but it was much more like venison, wild and a little dry. And during one short leave we returned to Holland to visit the Reichsmuseum and gape at Rembrandt's "Night Watch". Having seen only photographs in art books, the European masterpieces took us by surprise with their size or sometimes lack of it, and thrilled us with their power.

Being in Europe we two music lovers hoped to experience April in Paris, but we didn't reach the city of light until May. When Buz was scheduled for his spring leave, we arranged to visit June and Bud's good friends Lee and George Zinneman there. George was in Paris as Air Force Attaché to NATO, and he and Lee made us welcome in their handsome government issue apartment. We slept on a comfy mat on their living-room floor and there we conceived our first child! We kissed atop the "Awful Eiffel", climbed Montmartre while munching pomme fritte, (must eat French fries in France, of course!) visited the booksellers' booths on the left bank, learned to ask "Where is the Metro?" (Subway) in French, and dashed through enough of the Louvre to see Venus de Milo, the Mona Lisa and the glorious Winged Victory of Samothrace. There was no glass pyramid at the Louvre then, but L'Arc de Triomphe and the rushing taxis took our breath away. Then back we went to our little room in Germany, where it soon became apparent that I was to become a parent.

Buz had planned to apply for a government job so we could stay in Europe for a while, but I was getting steadily more homesick along with my morning sickness. Cutting short his hoped-for time as an expatriate on the continent was a big disappointment for Buz, and I must admit it was my fault!

On our final tourist venture before heading home we traveled through Austria to the Koenigsee with its onion domed chapels and great mountains rising from the lake. We went to Obersalzberg in Berchtesgarten, where Hitler's Berghof sat on a mountainside, and took snapshots of the General Walker Hotel, a US Army rest and recuperation center. Then we traveled on to Switzerland, with "little mother" feeling physically miserable and very pregnant, but quite thrilled to travel through the majestic Alps.

Chapter five
Playing house fifties style

In November we set sail for home on a small, crowded troop ship overflowing with soldiers and dependents. The food was barely palatable and we wives were put in quarters separate from our husbands. My morning sickness lasted all day for eight days, but joyfully, the USA awaited at the end of the journey. A tiny second floor apartment in Pennsauken, NJ, seemed almost grand after the room in Pirmasens, and we happily decorated a Charlie Brown Christmas tree with a dozen plastic snowflakes bought for fifty-nine cents.

Carrying wet laundry down the outside wooden stairs to hang it in the yard was a little tiring for a mother–to-be, and I dreamed of someday having one of those great inventions, a clothes dryer. Doc Dietrick had a funny story about the removal of some washing machines from the post laundry in San Antonio, where the new front-loading washers were always Bendix brand. He called the operation a Bendectomy. When preparing for our baby, Buz and I put a small maple chest on top of a full-sized old bureau and painted it white to make a modern "chest-on-chest", then glued on colorful cutout wooden alphabet letters. In later years, I separated and refinished the two parts and after more than fifty years, the little maple chest is with me still as a stand for the TV and home to all my photos.

June Elaine was born in Camden's Cooper Hospital on February 11, 1955. My sister loved her own name, so I honored her in giving the name to my daughter. The middle name I took from a poem by Tennyson with the lines: Elaine the fair, Elaine the lovable, Elaine the Lily maid of Astolat. It was a long labor, and in those days no husbands, no sisters or mothers were allowed to stay with the woman during her travails. I did know one of the nurses, a girl who had been my neighbor at Road's End, but she couldn't stay with me either. At last our little beauty was born, but by then my breasts were so engorged, there seemed to be no nipples, and she couldn't nurse. It looked like the poor dear would soon suffer dehydration.

My sister June was with her husband, Major Dietrick, stationed at Mountain Home Air Force Base in Idaho, and she couldn't come home to be with me. Luckily, Major D. secured passage on a flight to New Jersey and arrived at Cooper Hospital in the nick of time. Staff at the hospital had given the baby no water, hoping to force her to the breast, and then they decided to arbitrarily put my little love on formula, and allow my milk to dry up. Doc Dietrick wrote orders to give the baby sugar water, preventing dehydration, and to start my milk flowing with a breast pump. Huzzah! With this good start, I nursed baby June successfully until she was old enough to be weaned to the cup.

After a few months Meme offered daycare for our baby so I could go back to work at the bank. She and Papa gave us the gift of a plot of land beside their Cherry Hill home, on which we could build a house. They made us welcome in their home for the duration, giving us free housing until our place could be built. The lot was a beautiful wooded acre, but perk tests to guarantee drainage all failed, making it impossible to get a building permit. My parents then generously took out a loan and gave us the down payment for the purchase of a house. We found our dream home in Pennsauken, just five miles away.

The Dietrick babies were boys, Larry 3, David 1, so beautiful blue-eyed Junie was the princess in the family. She played dress-up and paraded in Meme's collection of hats, and gloried in the songs about buttons and bows that her grandmother made up for her. When Aunt June and Uncle Doc came home from the service and Doc opened his pediatric practice in Mt. Holly, she played with her cousins, captivated her aunt and uncle, and sealed her position as the girl in the family. Junie loved to stay at Aunt June and Uncle Doc's house, but her luck was not good on some of her visits. Once, she tumbled from bed, landing chin first on the bare floor and her sweet little face needed stitches provided by Uncle Doc in his office downstairs. A year or so later, she ran too fast behind a wagon while playing with the cousins and fell on that same pointed little chin. Bud stitched her up again, fearing she would never forgive him. Not really a problem, everyone forever adored Uncle Doc.

Another of Junie's unfortunate accidents happened when we were spending the weekend with the grandparents. Grandma Mid and Grandpa Oscar were still living in their Plainfield house in north-central Jersey, and we visited back and forth fairly often. June, barely a toddler, was using an early model walker called a Taylor Tot, and an open cellar door beckoned. Through the open door she made an unscheduled descent into the basement, riding the little cart. Thankfully, there were no broken bones nor concussions, but Grandma Mid panicked while Mom quietly and swiftly removed the baby to an upstairs bedroom. A phone call to Bud for immediate medical advice, then a stop at his office on the way home provided care for the baby and a tranquilizer (after the fact and at doctor's suggestion) for her mother.

Our home in Pennsauken had a sun-porch in front, looking out on pink and white dogwood trees and a sleepy tree-lined suburban street. In both the front and back yards we planted flower borders lush with coral-bells and Stargazer lilies. A small tree near the back fence looked to be ideal for climbing. Buz began working toward becoming a CPA, but he also joined me in the usual homeowners' do-it-yourself projects and enjoyed his hobbies of gardening and building a village for his HO gage trains. As we redesigned and redecorated, the house became ever more attractive, and easily lent itself to entertaining. One hugely successful party we held was South Sea Islands themed, with Tiki torches lighting the way through the snow into the house, and tiny fish-shaped crackers (an innovation at the time) swimming round the fifties comfort food that was universally served. I made the kitchen into an expression of myself, painting the cabinets blue, and covering the walls with "Contac" in a blue Delft pattern. Then I made a little desk on the countertop, where I could see out the window while I wrote my poems and observations or read.

Posing by the built-ins I designed.

Homes in this part of Merchantville and Pennsauken were comfortable and pleasant, lacking only one thing to make them perfect—swimming pools. We began neighborhood meetings and soon formed a cooperative to purchase land and build a swim club. For $100 a family, we became member/owners of a community pool and bathhouse. Once the Merchantville Swim Club was operational we swam regularly throughout the summer, enjoying the fellowship of the young families who were co-members and our chief social connection. The corny comment most frequently heard in post office and supermarket was, "I didn't recognize you with your clothes on". A Swim Club fund-raiser held at Camden County Music Circus was a production of *West Side Story*. Some folks were scandalized, claiming the storyline was too racy, but the 'fifties had its share of torrid tales. In 1956 Grace Metalias wrote the blatantly sexual *Peyton Place* and just about everyone read it—usually behind closed doors.

One of my more profitable interests or hobbies was sewing. I made most of my maternity clothes and sometimes our Christmas gifts. One year, I made matching red velveteen vests for the whole Dietrick family. Much later, I graduated to making coats for my daughters and myself, complete with inset buttonholes. Meme suffered from arthritis, and to keep her hands from stiffening she began to hook rugs. She became so skilled at Early American rug hooking and design that she was soon featured in books and crafts journals, and began taking courses to become an accredited teacher. She taught the craft for many years, and when she moved to Medford her classes were largely comprised of doctors' wives. The standing joke was her so innocently referring to these elegant ladies as her hookers.

We had a yellow German shepherd named Goliath, and a cat or two in the Pennsauken house, but the kitties fade from memory along with our less than scintillating dinner conversations. In the fall of '56 I resigned from the bank, announcing our intention to enlarge the Somers family. To the surprise and delight of my banking buddies, I kept my pledge. Mark was born in Burlington County Memorial Hospital, Mt. Holly, on Fathers Day, June 16, 1957.

Chapter six
Enter stage left

Another beautiful baby! Mark was plagued with colic as an infant, but grew into the sweetest little boy in the county. When he was just a couple months old we took him to Sears and had pictures taken. He was so cute and the proofs so expressive, I decided to use them as a "hook" to get myself invited to be a contestant on a Philadelphia TV quiz show. I strung the photos together and captioned each one. Something like:

"I hear you're looking for quiz contestants…"
"I know just the gal for you".
"She's a pretty smart cookie, my Mom!"

I got the call. The studio staff told me ever since seeing my creative pitch they had been eagerly awaiting my arrival. The prize for the weekly winner was a VIP trip to New York City, and my mother told me she'd baby-sit when I won. (Not if I won, but when!) She'd told me early on, "You can do anything you put your mind to", and I've always believed her.

It was right around Christmas when we went to New York, and the city was resplendent in holiday garb. Buz and I stayed in a hotel room overlooking Central Park, enjoyed elegant dinners and dancing and a Broadway show—*The Music Man*. I was sorry to miss Robert Preston in the role of Harold Hill, but we enjoyed his replacement, Burt Parks, whose patent leather hair and fast-talking presentation made him a delightfully believable con man. While waiting for curtain time, we stopped off in a nearby cocktail lounge, and chatted with the bartender, who said I reminded him of a promising young actress appearing down the street, a gal named Carol Burnett, who had just opened in *Once Upon a Mattress*.

The Dietrick's third son had been born about seven months before Mark, completing our kids' trio of beloved cousins—Larry, David and Steven. As the youngest, Stevie thought of himself as Daddy's boy, and he had a proprietary interest in holding Dad's attention. When our two families vacationed together, Uncle Doc, pediatrician and lover of babies, made a big fuss over Mark, the family's newest tot, much to Steven's chagrin. Aware of the care his dad gave to the illnesses of the town's children, and needing to distract Daddy from this awful new cousin, Stevie dramatically sobbed, "I need a peel!" Happily, Dad understood, the jealousy was soon forgotten and Steve was once more secure in his role as Daddy's boy.

As a little guy, Mark feared the monsters in his closet, so at story time I called up a protective pet to help keep him safe. Hinkle the *hippopotomotomus* was blue, and lived beneath his bed. The happy critter dined on sauerkraut and strawberries and loved and protected my little boy! Hinkle always closed the closet door, so we could say goodnight to the monsters. I am reminded Hinkle came back years later to visit my first grandson and brought along a sister, Pinkle, for the first granddaughter. Unfortunately, Hinkle had no skills for protecting Mark from fevers. The poor child was subject to high temperatures whenever he became ill, and with the high temps came hallucinations. Once the fever raged so high Mark went into convulsions. As always, our doctor was on call. Uncle Doc wrote a prescription and had me put our boy in a tub of cool water to bring down his fever. Together we got through one more crisis.

Parenting has its hurdles. The children usually manage to sail through the crises, but mom and dad may stress out just trying to hold it all together. Bud used to tease me because I didn't fall apart or panic no matter the level of drama. Using irony, he'd fondly call me "hysterical mother", and laugh. This sobriquet dated from the crazy time when Grandma Mid "lost it" over June's tumble to the basement, while I stayed calm and in charge until the trouble passed.

As Mark grew he seemed to be always laughing and dashing about, making friends of everyone. The back yard swing set and the climbing tree were favorite spots for the children. Our boy's first encounter with a neighborhood bully left him confused and horrified. Accustomed to a life of smiles and an adoring family he was stung by the fact some child would actually belt him. Hitting just doesn't happen in our world! Would that every child could say as much.

June early learned her ABCs and numbers, and looked forward to being a big girl and going to school. We lived within easy walking distance of the local grade school, and when she started kindergarten, Mark and I walked with her to and from school. On the way, we met the Finleys, who had a girl in June's class and a boy who would be starting school at the same time as Mark. The mother, Ellen, soon became my dearest friend. She and her husband George were Buz's and my neighborhood buddies. Other close friends were our dentist and his wife, and my old high school friend and former sweetheart, Jack McDonnel, also a dentist, and his wife. The McDonnels had a summer place on Long Beach Island, where the beautiful Barnegat Light is to be found and we spent quality time together on the beaches there.

Mark enjoyed being an "only child" when June was at school. He would be my escort to the supermarket or the local haberdashery where we became friends with the charming gay shop manager. My boy suffered through trips to the brand new Cherry Hill Mall—the first all-season indoor shopping center in the country—built on the very fields where I rode horseback as a girl, and where I ate the world's most delicious homemade ice cream at the Fireside Cottage. When the time grew closer for him to begin school, Mark began to worry that there would be no one at home to "take care of" his Mom. Maybe we could have another baby?

My sister was known in the Isaksen family as the beauty, and I was considered the quiz kid or the personality. I told her once that I hated being called cute, and longed to someday be thought stunning like her. She laughed and said, "And I just wish they'd say, 'Mrs. Dietrick is such a cute little thing'". When I grew older, I mentally shrugged my shoulders and decided it was OK to be a non-beauty; I might even still be "cute" at seventy.

Near the Dietrick house, in Mount Holly there was a little drainage ditch where muddy overflow was channeled off the driveways and gardens of the neighborhood. One afternoon, when the boys were still quite young, June was going to the school for some event, walking with her middle son, David. As they started out along the sidewalk, he suggested instead his favorite short cut. "Let's go the other way", he said, "by the lovely place where the water flows". It's all in the perception, isn't it?

In typical 1950's fashion, I joined the Merchantville Junior League once we'd settled into our home. Admired seniors from the Women's Club mentored the young wives and mothers in the junior club, and served as models for aging with grace. With the opportunities the club programs provided, we began to take our place in the public arena, developing our skills along the paths of our individual interests and talents. My gift and area of interest was theatre, and I began acting in one-act tournaments across the state, eventually becoming State Drama Chairman. As Chair, it was my job to arrange for and host the state competitions—daylong events staged in a different town each year.

The Somers's first family car was a second-hand Plymouth, which fades quickly from my memory, where it never made much of an impact to begin with. Later vehicles carry much brighter mind-pictures. Our teal blue Ford Falcon convertible didn't come along till 1964, but that one I still recall with a warmly tingling heart! In October of 1962, I was chauffeuring a group of the clubwomen along Garden State Parkway in an unremembered auto, when news of the Cuban missile crisis blasted forth on the radio and gave us all a bad fright. We were sure we'd be plunged into war. Horn-toots of admiration from passing trucks, however, eased the tension and cheered us on. (Shapely knees seen from the driver's seat of an 18-wheeler were thought to be kind of racy in those days.) At the previous tournament, as I stood on stage and welcomed our sisters from across New Jersey, my future baby made itself known with a theatrical walk-on. The first time I "felt life" the little one was quite visible crossing beneath my elegant black maternity dress—on stage! Was this perhaps foreshadowing?

Thinking he might tend toward being tougher on sons than on daughters, Buz had put in his order for another girl. A blonde like her mother, this time, please. This special order pregnancy was a little tough on me, with constant heartburn and a siege of walking pneumonia, but the delivery was relatively smooth. Was I maybe getting the hang of this baby-making thing? In May of 1962, Mark contracted chickenpox, and just before Mothers Day our exquisite Kristi was born at Burlington County Memorial. When we brought her home to Pennsauken, her natural newborn state pretty nearly protected her from Mark's contagion. She got only one hot red pockmark, and a life-long immunity to chickenpox.

As Kristi reached her second year, my precious mother-in-law gave me a gift of true love. She arranged for Grandpa Oscar and herself to sponsor my education, enabling me to enroll at Rutgers University night classes at the Camden campus. Ellen Finley enrolled with me, and we protected each other on the dark streets, walking between the parking lot and the classes. Sociology, Economics, World History, Philosophy, Cultural Anthropology... What joy! And the professional writer who taught my English Composition class became my muse and my mentor, encouraging me to cultivate my uniqueness and express myself through my writing. In my journal I wrote:

She called him Maestro—he who pulled the bow

Across her spirit's taut and trembling strings.
His gentle fingers pressed upon her heart
And called the music forth, and gave her wings.
She loved him well, responding mind to mind,
With songs that left her changed,
transfigured, new;
Received and asked of him no more than this
One gift—herself—and to the sky she flew,
Saw beauty fresh and truth…and loneliness,
The price she'd pay for soaring, singing flight.
Aloft she realized that although free.
She was alone…alone at that great height.
Then as she listened to an inner voice
The music in her mind swelled and grew strong.
It carried her enlightened, back to earth,
Where all the world could hear and share her song.

One of the writing challenges for this inspirational class was to write a speech about our "concerns". As usual I chose to interpret the assignment a bit differently, and my speech became something of a credo. It began, "I call myself a Christian, but with Aristotle I believe…" And closed with, "Each of us comes into this world with unique and wonderful gifts. I believe it is my responsibility (my concern) to use my gifts well and to share them in the world. And to be always, in all ways, kind".

After hearing my presentation, a woman in the class said to me, "You're a Unitarian!" Startled and confused, I said, "I'm a what?" I had never before heard of Emerson's gentle faith, expressed in his writings and the Transcendentalist movement. So this kind woman brought me flyers about liberal religion and printed sermons from her minister, the

Rev. Ed Lane in Cherry Hill. Discovering in someone else's words my own beliefs and philosophy, I knew I had found my church home, and there I was soon to be found every Sunday. About this time, I realized that a thirty-year-old woman probably ought not to be known as "Taffy", so I reeducated everyone to call me "DJ".

I have never believed in corporal punishment. I simply did not like the idea of spanking my children so I talked with them instead, and as adults they sometimes insist the words, "I'm disappointed in you", hurt worse than a slap. There was one exception to my no spanking rule, however. It had to do with risk to life and limb. One day June and Mark made the very bad mistake of playing on the railroad tracks near our house. Little Kristi was with them, and my discovery of their dangerous behavior unglued me so badly I paddled them both. The crux of the tale is that my beautiful three-year-old presented herself for spanking along with her big brother and sister. After all, she had been on the tracks, too. So to assuage her injured pride, I faked it with a painless paddling.

I remember very little about my grandmother, Jetta. She slides through my memory as a serious person, and I know my father's connection with her never seemed very strong. His brother Herb, who was an alcoholic, occupied most of her love and concern, and once grown, Papa was not given much materially or emotionally. Besides which, he'd married an outsider, while Herb's wife was a Norwegian girl. When Jetta died, she left everything to Herb; except for one thing Papa loved dearly, an old wrought iron-framed mirror. He remembered it from his boyhood, when it was brightly decorated with the Norwegian royal heraldry and held pride of place in his mother's Bay Ridge, Brooklyn flat. He said she had been given the mirror among some affects from a building he called the "Copper Mansion" in New York City, the home of an expatriate Norwegian baron of industry.

By the time the mirror came into Papa's possession the frame had been painted over with green enamel and gilt. He took it to work, removed the glass, stripped it and re-fired it so it was all black wrought iron. While working in the city I went to the Norwegian Consulate in Philadelphia, and researched the royal heraldry, then came home and painted the flags and armor on the frame in authentic colors and design, and Papa reinserted the mirror. The old treasure was not up to my mother's standards of good taste, however. She called it "that thing" and wouldn't give it house room. So one day Papa showed up at my house in Pennsauken with the mirror wrapped in brown paper, and presented it to me. It would henceforth represent my "in residence" state wherever I might live, traveling to any new home with me, not with the movers.

At some point, long after the mirror came to reside with me, I looked into the glass and saw what at first appeared to be the surface badly in need of cleaning. Looking into the mirror more carefully, I saw within the glass the face of a Viking with heavy brows, goatee and winged helmet. We decided to call the illusion Cousin Olav, the family ghost. The children love him and I'm happy to say that even Papa saw Olav, when he visited us in Fullerton. The image seems to be more clearly discerned in locations where Olav and I are most happy.

The "Cousin Olav" mirror.

One of Buz and the kids' favorite meals was my mild, slightly sweet chili. Once when we visited the Plainfield grandparents, Grandma Mid thoughtfully made the dish she had heard they loved and the poor dear was sadly disappointed when none of them would eat her lovingly prepared dish. It just wasn't like Mom's. The secret ingredient in my chili, meatloaf, and spaghetti is applesauce, and the truly magical ingredient—the one that makes it "real" food by Amy's definition—is love. One way I expressed my love was by offering the children food they really liked, for instance, leaving out the beans in June's and Amy's chili and giving them rice instead, because that's what tasted good to them. Mark never had to eat mushrooms or eggplant, and Kristi got to enjoy my creamy potato soup and chicken salad. Being given the food they loved, they each knew they were important, respected and listened to. It was a kindness, like my mother's arranging to have fresh green beans whenever I came for dinner. We love to feed those we love, giving them the gift of life.

It was the sixties and I can't explain the stress that developed in my marriage during this time. So many years later, it seems overly dramatic and unnecessary, and I wonder why I didn't do things differently. But I believe all my yesterdays have brought me to this day, and I know this day is good.

Buz's accountant boss disapproved of my decision to study at the university in a time when girls usually went to college to earn their M-r-s rather than a PhD. He said I would educate myself out of the mainstream and soon have no one to talk to. He may have referred to "Lodge and Cabot", (In Boston it was said, "The Cabots speak only to the Lodges, and the Lodges speak only to God".) Perhaps he was more insightful than I realized, as talking with Buz became more and more difficult, and I became more and more educated and more and more sophisticated, critical, judgmental and unaccepting.

When Kristi was old enough to come along, taking my love of theatre a bit further, I went to work with the Second Story Studio, a light-hearted and enthusiastic troupe of actors creating children's theatre in Philadelphia. I was hired to MC the shows, portraying a sweet new image of Mother Goose (think Julie Andrews without the singing). Sewing maven that I was, I made my own costume—blue, my favorite color, and floor length, with puff sleeves and a long apron decorated in ribbons and colorful plastic measuring spoons. A basket hung over my arm, nesting the goose puppet on my right hand and I wore a big straw hat trimmed with multi-colored flowers and feathers. We were booked into the John B. Kelly Playhouse in the Park, in Philadelphia's Fairmount Park for the summer season. Mine was a Fran Allison type role in a human and puppet partnership not unlike that of Kukla, Fran and Ollie. We'd do our little puppet show outside the theatre tent (it was theatre in the round) providing pre-show entertainment before I went onstage to introduce the overture and prepare the audience for the show. At each performance, I invited the children having birthdays to join me onstage for a congratulatory song, and at every show my 3-year-old starlet joined the birthday kiddies. The stage was her natural home.

Our theatre company included Dally Mohamed, a big black and beautiful darling who could belt a song and deliver a funny line like the best of Broadway. Our triple or should I say quadruple threat writer, singer, dancer, actor—Don Kersey— was a genius at creating scripts and songs that delighted the grown-ups while holding the children enthralled. Junie and Mark adored everyone in the cast, but it was especially beautiful to see our handsome little blond guy perched on the lap of one of these two friends with their lovely brown faces and great warm hearts

From children's theatre I moved on to become Director of Group Sales at the Camden County Music Circus and when in residence at the theatre, took my little diva with me. My desk was across from the box office and Miss Kristi, exercising her first attempts at printing, copied the letters to form her first written words: BOX OFFICE. Two of the artists we enjoyed meeting were Robert Goulet and Wayne Newton. Newton's appearance at the Music Circus was particularly memorable for us because our little blonde bombshell left her seat in the audience during his performance, and barreled down the aisle to join him onstage. As she hit the stage, he dropped down on one knee and welcomed her into his arms! Yet again a sign of theatrical things to come.

The summer Kristi was four we rented a vacation apartment on Long Beach Island, near Barnegat Light, and one afternoon our upstairs neighbor let his dog loose in the yard against local ordinances. Another dog on leash came trotting past and soon there was a huge ruckus and two dogs ready for a fight. When the neighbor restrained his angry dog our Kristi joyfully went over to greet the animal, which had not yet calmed down from his confrontation. He snarled and bit her in the face, just missing her eye. We called the emergency squad and they took off with us down the island to the only doctor, several towns away for stitches and a tetanus shot. My heart broke holding my little beauty in my arms as the car raced along. Somehow, we all got through the crisis, and amazingly Kristi never lost her deep-seated love of dogs. Who knew?

Always, my love of theatre guided my activities, and I found myself adapting a script and directing the Methodist Church's youth in a production of "The Littlest Angel". I was working with the associate minister, Irving Stevens, and his humor and sweetness lit a spark between us. That spark would ignite a flame.

Buz never shared my love of the theatre nor what Barry Manilow calls "clever conversation". Communication at home had become more and more difficult, disagreements increased and most nights ended with me in tears, though I can't remember exactly why. Finally, I took the children to my parents' house and told my husband our marriage was over. I filed for divorce, and Attorney Alfred Powell, a classmate from Mt. Holly made the process fairly easy. But it was never painless. The little ones and I moved to an apartment in Merchantville and I continued selling group theatre parties. I contracted with an answering service to avoid missed calls, and though I never met her, became telephone friends with Mary, the voice of my business. Our inside joke was about what was acceptable for a lady to "show". I told her that good legs were great to show, but the skin above the tops of my stockings shouldn't be seen because that would be "tacky". Somehow that word tickled Mary and made her laugh. When the phone rang during mealtime at our apartment, June and Mark would remind me to stay seated, eat my dinner and let the answering service do the talking. "That's what you pay them for, Mom".

Irving left the church and his family, and moved to Burlington County where he began working as a teacher. My first poem to my colleague and mentor, Irving Stevens, was this:

Hello friend.
How few have merited from me this proud salute.
There is a sweet and pungent flavor to the words,
Born of my recognition of a kindred mind,
My secret awareness that here is one
Who will know me and be known,
One who will speak with me of soaring things
And leave the dull and the pedestrian behind.
Each of us is a creature quite apart, a unique spirit;
Yet there is a joy beyond all other joys
In that special oneness true friends know.
Hello, friend.

Soon he was coming to Merchantville to visit me and play with the children. His kindness and wit and his funny sayings endeared him to us all, and before long Mark "proposed". "Mom", he said, "Would you marry Mr. Stevens?"

Chapter seven
A place in history

A new life. While living in Merchantville, I interviewed for a new, non-theatre job. I met with an old friend from school days, the editor of the *Mt. Holly Herald*. He hired me as women's news editor and feature writer for *Burlington County Publishing's News Press*—four weekly papers. The papers covered four New Jersey towns along the Delaware River: Burlington, Riverside, Palmyra and Levittown, (now retro-named Willingboro Township). Local news for each town had its own layout, and county news was the same in all four newssheets.

I discovered that experiences were heightened for me whenever I was preparing to write about them, and some peculiarity of my mind allowed me to "get to the nut" of any interview quickly and easily. My writing style was clearly identifiable from my lead paragraph, and folks along the Delaware River soon came to recognize my work with or without a byline. As to bylines, I wrote under two names. The women's news editor (Yes, they thought it necessary to separate out the homey stuff for the ladies!) used "Doris Jeanine", and the feature writer was "D. J. Somers", giving the impression we had a larger staff, and clouding the gender of the feature reporter. I wrote headlines and cutlines (under photos), a column called "The View From My Window" and a series about education along the river, and though I couldn't type worth a darn, my editor loved my writing and I loved my job.

On one assignment, Mark came with me to interview the town's Welcome Wagon hostess, and that ten-year-old budding writer actually wrote the piece I used in the paper. His article was better than most of the releases that crossed my desk, and might only be spotted as a youthful effort by his writing "her boy" when he meant the woman's son. My first paid-for published work outside a newspaper was a story for *Burlington County Magazine* about Matt Sleeper, who, as a planning commissioner, was bringing some new industry into the county. I'd known Matt in high school, and enjoyed introducing him to my readers countywide.

My connection to the Unitarian Church in Cherry Hill grew stronger, and I invited Irving to Sunday services and to a "Why I Am a Unitarian" discussion group. The minister, Ed Lane, suggested Irv apply for ministerial fellowship with the Unitarian Universalist Association, since he was already an ordained minister. Having absorbed the widely accepted image of Unitarians as "The thinking people", he told Ed, "I don't believe I can do that. I'm no intellectual". Ed's response, "You've got DJ". With my support, Irving applied to become a Unitarian Universalist minister. He met the Rev. Robert Jordan Ross, recruiter for the UUA Department of Ministry, and learned what books he had to read and what criteria he would have to meet to become a UU minister. We in the Cherry Hill church were proud of "our minister", Ed Lane, when he quickly answered the call from Dr. Martin Luther

King to join the march on Selma. The great tragedy of that courageous rally was the murder of his friend and Unitarian colleague, the Rev. James Reeb.

Stevens's wedding cake.

Irving and I had accepted Mark's "proposal", and planned to marry when Irv's divorce became final. His wife had traveled to Alabama to obtain a prompt decree, but we had no idea how long the process would take. Ed Lane was called to serve the Westport, Connecticut, UU church, and he volunteered to officiate at our wedding in that glorious venue. His wife, Ann, hosted a little family reception for us. Sadly the family didn't include my parents, sister or uncle, as I had become *persona non grata* when I decided to marry Irving Stevens, whom they saw as "the other man". For my wedding day, December 16, 1967, I had a silver-grey hand-knit suit made and a pink angora pillbox hat. (Thank you, Jackie Kennedy.) My three lovely children made up the wedding party. Irving and I honeymooned in a Martha's Vineyard cottage borrowed from Kristi's preschool teacher. Even the cold was delicious!

Before he completed his fellowshipping requirements, Irving was called as minister to the Universalist Church in Stafford, the oldest Universalist church gathered in Connecticut. It was once served by Hosea Ballou II, and later by Daniel and Mary Livermore, giants in the history of Universalism. The little village of Stafford or Stafford Hollow, was set in a small basin at the foot of a hill, anchored by an ancient millpond and a tiny post office. "Downstreet" (Staffordese for downtown) was Stafford Springs, where the schools and shops and the bigger churches were to be found. On the far edge of town was Big Bunny Market (a we-sell-everything superstore, long before Walmart) with its huge rabbit icon atop the building.

The parsonage was a big beautiful old colonial place with the church's assembly room in one wing. The front door opened onto a wide center hallway leading to an elegant staircase. On the right was the study, where we set up our seven-foot partners' desk, and on the left was the parlor. Down the hall a door to the assembly room opened on the right and another to the kitchen on the left. A pantry nestled at the rear of the kitchen and a butler's pantry held pride of place between kitchen and parlor. While still in Jersey we had acquired "Missy" an enthusiastic German shepherd mix Irv loved to chase in circles from the parsonage kitchen to pantry to parlor to hallway to kitchen and around again. We never lacked for entertainment! Upstairs there were three bedrooms and a little sewing room, opening onto the main hall. A fourth bedroom (Kristi's) over the assembly room wing had a view of the millpond below, and an awareness of the next-door stairs to the attic above. A large dollhouse built by Papa for the girls lived in her closet. At the end of the side hall was our family TV room. As the youngest, it was Kristi's turn to have a fear of monsters, and hers dwelt in the attic. Ah, childhood!

Our little church meetinghouse, a short walk from the parsonage, was right out of a Currier and Ives print—white clapboard with a small bell tower. There was a kind of picture frame on the front lawn in which we displayed passages from the Wayside Pulpit, usually a quote from Thoreau or Emerson, Theodore Parker or William Ellery Channing. The congregation was ruled by a coterie of elderly folk led by a maiden lady who had taught school for fifty years and held the purse strings as church treasurer for forty. It was 1967 and we blew in on the winds of change. Our gift to the Stafford Church was an influx of young families, but that gift changed the nature of the congregation forever. These were people who were ready to bring in new ideas and grow. We still held the traditional covered dish suppers in the church basement, but the young ones also called us and each other frequently to say, "What are you having for dinner? We're having such and such. We'll bring it over and have an impromptu potluck". The group became very close.

The village postmaster was an alcoholic, as was at least one of the young husbands among the newer members in our growing church. Mr. Postmaster and Mr. Parishioner did show up for services each Sunday, but smelling strongly of alcohol.

One family became very dear to us because of their five boys, especially Andy and Linc. Andy and our Mark became so close they spoke of themselves as "twin brothers with different mothers". And Lincoln won my heart with his intense awareness. He was the middle child of the five, all vying for attention. Each had his own way of catching your eye—just being oldest, getting in trouble, excelling in sports or study, getting sick. And then there was Linc, who related. He saw me. He knew if I changed my part or wore a new blouse, he looked at me when he talked with me, and he saw me. Such a gift of love!

Mark commented on a Wayside Pulpit message quoting William Ellery Channing, "Let you life speak more loudly than your lips". Noting that this was the opposite of the message some friends got from their parents: "Do as I say, not as I do". Ah, yes! A wise fellow at so young an age! I had certain agreements with my children. They knew our home was always open for their friends, and meals could usually be shared, but it was to be an automatic "no" if they asked "Can my friend stay for dinner?" in front of the friend. Just check with Mom on the QT first and it's almost certainly a yes. If, however you are invited somewhere you don't want to go, just phrase your parental request like this: "Mom, I can't go to (wherever) can I?" You will receive a resounding and supportive "No!"

Camping with our kitchen box.

We purchased a Cox Camper, which looked like a low cream-colored box trailing behind the family car. When the camper was opened, a curved tent top, reminiscent of a covered wagon, appeared over two built-in beds. Irv made a wonderful kitchen box with storage space for all our non-perishables and a front door that dropped down to become a work counter. There were screw-in legs and a place for everything—pots, dishes and flatware along with the canned goods and cereals. We had a separate tent for the kids, and we all became ardent campers. Irving was the experienced one, always taking care of us. Many of our outings took us to beach towns like those on Cape Cod or the Rhode Island shore, and we camped at Ferry Beach in Maine where I learned to belly dance a little, to make silver jewelry a little, and to journal a lot. When we were at home, the camper rested in the driveway, and in summer we opened it up as a place for Irv and me to read and relax.

We called it the parsonage annex and had the phone outside on a very long cord.

Sermons were a shared challenge for the Stevens team. Irving, the experienced minister, came up with the concepts, I drew on my writing skills to put them on paper, and he delivered them. He taught me so much about ministry by being a good pastor and a willing companion himself. His jovial "Sure!" in response to any invitation (usually for a cup of coffee) cheered everyone, and reminded me that drinking coffee with a church member was part of the job, and not some Puritan sin of laziness. He taught me to mellow out, and to sit down from time to time, even if I had to learn to knit argyles to keep myself seated. If he had to dash off to the store, for instance, he'd insist I come along. "What do we gain if you stay home and keep working?" he asked. "A few minutes saved, but they're minutes we'd rather be spending together". That togetherness dismayed some of our New England gossips, making snide storytelling unlikely to impossible, and it may even have led to our next great achievement, our baby girl.

This was a pleasant pregnancy, with other women in the congregation in various stages of expectation as well. June was thrilled at the prospect of a baby in the family, and Mark, at 12, was concerned about my well-being. He named the future sibling Todd, and helped to redecorate the sewing room and convert it into a nursery. The window in the little room opened onto the porch roof, and I remember him dancing on that roof and helping clean the window to let the sunshine in. A "New Ministers' (and wives) Seminar" was scheduled in Boston in mid-October, 1969, and looking at my due date, I told the Rev. Dr. Joe Barth, Director of the Department of Ministry, we'd be there—with a new baby. He was skeptical but hopeful, and then surprised. (Re-reading this, I'm struck by how natural the "and wives" was for that era, when the spouses were nearly never male.) When our "Todd" arrived on October second, the day before my birthday, she needed a prompt name change. June and Mark chose to name her Amy after a character in their favorite TV show, "Dark Shadows". I added her middle name and a slice of history. My mother had seen Mae Desmond in a play or film called "Lilac Time" and she fell in love with the song, "Jeanine, I Dream of Lilac Time", so gave me the middle name Jeanine. I have always loved the name, and chose to share it with my new baby girl.

Mark may have shed a tear or two because his expected brother was a girl, but once he held her, Amy was his darling. Less than a week after she was born she was on the way to being the darling of all Stafford Springs, where we toted the 3-day old baby in a "Pumpkin Seat" (a predecessor of the car-seat) to the Big Bunny, the Post Office, and up and down Main Street. By week's end we were on our way to 25 Beacon Street, Boston, where she won the hearts of all the clergy and clergy wives. Our best friends, Frank and Evie Taylor, had a boy around the same time, and named him Andrew. His older brother was Jeffrey. Boys were born into several other church families as well, but our little goddess was the only girl.

Our old fashioned parsonage with its classy butler's pantry, provided a unique arrangement for a small baby. The service counter under the window was wide enough to be used as a changing table and the open space before the china cabinets easily accommodated her bathinette. Our little girl developed a sense of humor and an instinct for mischief before her sixth month. When I had her on the changing space, I dared not turn away to reach behind me for a diaper, because the little mischief would reach out her foot as if to fall, and when I jumped to save her.... laugh!

Although my parents and sister had not been willing to talk to me since I married Irving, I continued to send birthday cards, Christmas wishes and little notes of love. I sometimes awoke in tears from dreams of family. When my baby arrived, I knew what I must do. On a visit to New Jersey after Amy's birth, I took her and the other three children to Medford, and rang my mother's doorbell. When she answered the door, I placed my baby girl in her grandmother's arms, and the family was healed. Meme could never resist a baby!

Stafford was an idyllic setting, and our own Tom Sawyer found his Huck Finn in the neighboring family across the road. The Delanies had enough children to supply playmates for our whole clan, and Mark became great pals with Tim, the eldest male. The boys hung out in the parsonage barn or explored the creek leading to the millpond, built a raft to cross over to their hidden island, and rode along with us to the community's social gathering place, the town dump. Mark tells me the raft sank immediately upon hitting the water, but the boys finally got it to float after finding some empty oil drums to use as pontoons. They got these treasures at the dump, of course, where a sign warned, "Trash must be assorted". We never worried about our young adventurers, because they always came home promptly when Dad whistled for them.

Just up the hill from the Delainies lived "Peachy" an old dear with a love of pets and children, who provided a comforting non-church connection for the minister's wife. An outside ear was an important part of my survival, and Peachy was a loving listener. Surely among the most difficult of careers in that day, being wife to a clergyman was a no-win combination of expectations and prohibitions. Expected to be model homemaker and parent, yet not too successful, unpaid congregational servant, Sunday School teacher, secretary, and community liaison, but never too visible, she mustn't be too attractive, but always appealing. And so on. While in Stafford, I wrote for the denominational newspaper, The UU World, and provided an occasional article for the local paper, did some substitute teaching in elementary and junior high classes and, along with Irving, and the Taylors, hand-carved flaming chalice medallions to sell at UU General Assemblies.

Chapter eight
Teenagers rule!

Since I had an abundance of church jobs without the rewards, I decided to enter the UUA DRE (director of religious education) accreditation program, and began studying many of the same materials required for ministry. I attended classes at Crane Seminary at Tufts University outside Boston, and workshops at Meadville Lombard School of Theology in Chicago, participated in CPE (clinical pastoral education) at the Norwalk State Mental Hospital, and in the course of my studies became a proponent of open education.

Working with the youth of the church to put together their own worship service, I suggested they forgo great abstract themes, like love and peace, and build their presentation around something specific—what do you want from us, the adults? They responded with enthusiasm and with four requests:

1. Listen to us.
2. Take us seriously.
3. Tell us the truth.
4. Trust us.

What a guide for parents! Who wouldn't make these same requests in all our relationships? I believe talking with me, not to me or at me, is the best expression of these gifts. And lies "to protect the children" or to keep them innocent do neither. They simply set a bad example. With the help of Evie Taylor and the other young Universalist families, we opened our own "Free School" at the church. This was an open curricula program, where the projects combined various disciplines and students moved at their own pace. It worked beautifully for inquisitive thoughtful students, but for the lazy ones, not so much.

Irving wasn't big on do-it-yourself projects, but he became fascinated with refinishing furniture. The greatest of his "finds" was a red drop-leaf kitchen table that had been abandoned in the parsonage attic. Once the red paint was removed, it turned out to be solid oak, and as I looked at the long legs and short leaves, my artist's eye demanded an adjustment. "It would look really good", I said, "if you just shorten the legs. We could make it into a coffee table!" Irv thought it a crazy idea, but chose to humor me. That table was the center of our family living room fun and my platform for making announcements for more than twenty-five years!

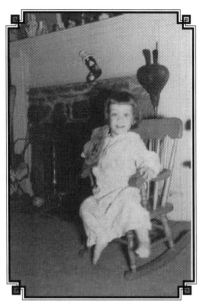

Junie and the cozy rocker

The other piece of furniture that graced our lives and cozied our bottoms through the years had arrived about the time of June's first Christmas. It was a warm maple child-sized rocking chair that each of the children used and loved in their turn. Even high school-aged youngsters and slim adults squeezed between its wooden arms for the special hug that rocker bestowed, and each of the siblings knew in their hearts that it belonged to them alone.

Before the historic Supreme Court decision on Roe vs. Wade, Irving and I became members of the Connecticut Clergy Counselors for Problem Pregnancies. We explored alternatives with women who might or might not decide that abortion was the answer to their problem. Our resources included out-of-state physicians in places where abortion was legal, and methods for transporting the women to them. We were surprised to discover that most of our clients were not young girls "in trouble", but married women, usually physically and/or mentally and financially depleted by too many pregnancies and large families of children. During our training session, we were given a gestation chart, with which to calculate the time of conception and the expected time of delivery in a normal pregnancy. Irv sat studying the document, then turned to me and grinned. "Honey", he said, "Not only was Amy a birthday present; she was a Christmas present!"

The death of Stafford's Postmaster was a learning experience in ministry for me. Joe's family had become accustomed to the steady drinking he did after work causing him to pass out at the dinner table, so his final farewell was not really noticed until he fell to the floor—literally "dead" drunk. His wife, Ann, called the parsonage immediately, and Irving and I went at once to minister to her and her sons in their grief and anger. Joe's face was blue as he lay on the kitchen floor; his body awaiting the arrival of the emergency squad, and for us, the work of mending a damaged family began. Ann was appointed Postmistress to replace Joe, and slowly the family began to heal.

My first husband had remarried and with the birth of his daughter Kate, started a second family. Mark, June and Kristi were able to visit with them from time to time and they were coming to know one another better when tragedy struck. Buz had been born prematurely, and his mother died of toxemia shortly after his birth. Although Mid, the woman his dad married when Buz was three, adored him and was beloved by him and seemed always his true mother, he carried the burden of his birthmother's death all through his life. At barely forty he was struck down by a brain tumor, leaving behind a lovely widow and young daughter.

Around the time of the Kent State massacre Irving and I were invited to be co-directors of the UU High School youth camp at Rowe, Massachusetts. Amy was ten months old when we took the family along the Mohawk Trail to the denomination's campground in the Berkshires. On the way, we bought a tapestry throw rug with horses pictured on it for our baby girl to crawl upon, and we settled into a new phase of our own religious education. In the summer of 1970 and those that followed the teens were still children of the sixties, brimming with creativity, music and tie-dye. We encouraged community building at camp, but we didn't require anyone to attend all the workshops, because our young songwriters, poets and deep thinkers sometimes needed quiet time just sitting on the porch and rocking to germinate their next masterpiece.

My parents had given me some precious gifts and lessons for living. They taught me hospitality, dignity, affection and humor. And from my mother I learned to behave "like a lady" throughout my life. New gifts of learning came from the sweet teens of Rowe Camp who introduced us to *The Little Prince* and *Jonathan Livingston Seagull.* These youngsters (my people!) taught me to be flexible and mellow, to freely give and treasure hugs and to express my creativity. But most of all they taught me self-acceptance. Who could forget three summers of climbing Blueberry Hill to pick the fruit, hiking down from camp to the old chapel for youth-led worship services, ghost stories or a game of "murder", designing and building stained glass windows, eating green eggs and ham or blueberry muffins and singing *Dona Nobis Pacem* before a meal, or those late night girly talks, when 10-year-old Kristi listened in and commented, "I didn't know a back rub was the 'first step'".

After almost five years in Stafford, Irving and I interviewed with a pulpit committee from the Bangor Unitarian Church in Maine, and they called us as a team to be their minister and associate.

Chapter nine
Yea, team!

The folks at the Bangor Unitarian Church had just gone through an intense long-range planning process with an outside consultant, to prepare for their future. The consultant team was made up of Josiah Bartlett, a retired Unitarian minister who later served as President of Starr King School of the Ministry, and his wife Laile. As a result of their surveys, guidance and parish interviews the Bangor church decided to call a husband and wife team, clarifying the wife's role as a member of the church staff. There would be none of the traditional unappreciated demands on the minister's wife!

Almost immediately upon our arrival in Bangor we became embroiled in a confrontation with the religious right. The fundamentalist Christian pastor, Buddy Herman, a Jerry Fallwell wannabe, wrote a letter to the editor of the daily paper objecting to the staging of *Jesus Christ, Superstar* in the Bangor Civic Auditorium, the usual venue for large theatrical productions. He admitted he had never seen it, nor heard the music nor read the libretto, but he knew it was blasphemy, giving us an easy target. The "new minister" and his associate at the Bangor Unitarian Church responded in support of artistic freedom, pointing out that artists throughout history have pictured the Christ as they saw Him in their own creative minds. We stirred up a bit of interest to be sure.

The American Unitarian Association and the Universalist Church of America had joined together to form the Unitarian Universalist Association of Congregations in 1961. (Thomas Starr King proposed such a union in 1860). While most member churches in the UUA by now identified themselves with both names, the two congregations in Bangor chose to retain their original singular identities. The Universalist Church across town also retained its more conservative public image. Irving and I had learned early on that in our UU tradition, "the church" is the people gathered, and the building in which the people meet is called the meetinghouse. Bangor Unitarian prided itself on being one of the churches served by Ralph Waldo Emerson during his tenure as a called minister. The parsonage sat cozily across the street from the Hannibal Hamlin house, where Abraham Lincoln's Vice President, a member of our church, once lived. And the meetinghouse, a classic red brick landmark with a tall white steeple and bell tower visible from well outside the city, stood across from the Bangor House Hotel at the corner of Union and Main Streets. Adjacent to the church building on the Main Street side was our ancient parish house, home to the Sunday school, meeting and assembly rooms, the ministers' study and a good sized kitchen. In the meetinghouse heavy pews facing a high pulpit covered the huge interior space without hope of being filled. A lovely pipe organ and choir loft almost disappeared in the rear of the dark hall.

Part of the congregation's agreed-upon long range plan was the renovation of the building to make it more user friendly, so it became our job to prepare the people for that process. We visited families and individuals one by one, and really talked with everyone about the proposed changes. The architects were brilliant; their designs for the arrangement of our interior space would give us a fresh new start, literally turning the church around. Because we "did our homework" the church moved forward with the plan without the kind of conflict change so often brings. All the pews were removed and comfortable stacking chairs brought in to provide flexibility of arrangement. A small low stage with a moveable podium was built beneath the choir loft, so that what had been the back of the room became the front. A ten foot high dividing wall separated the sanctuary from the rest of the building without shutting off the view of our great high ceiling. Beyond this partition were dividing walls that formed the new ministers' study, an extra room (which became known as Amy's office) a meeting room, and a kitchen, as well as unisex restrooms. The overall effect was stunningly beautiful! The old parish house became our resource for community service, providing meeting space for Alcoholics Anonymous, NAACP, a Gay Rights group, craft fairs, church fundraisers and various city-wide events.

By now June was a senior in high school, and as throughout her school years, was beloved by her teachers. Though she was not a scholar, she completed assignments, was dependable, friendly and well behaved—a model student. She even enjoyed her high school years so much she took advantage of an unusual Bangor High option to stay on for an extra year after graduation. June was the premier audience, always laughing at the siblings' antics and ever appreciative of their performances. Her own preference as a performer was singing in choirs and choral groups whenever the opportunity arose.

She made friends throughout the city, including the gay fellows who were not universally accepted in Bangor.

Having found their comfort zone at Rowe Camp, our kids seemed to ride fairly smoothly through the challenge of being "PKs" (preachers' kids). They willingly and actively took part in the church youth group and participated with them in presenting creative worship services. We tell a joke on ourselves as Unitarian Universalists, about one of us entering the afterlife. It is said he died and was on his way…somewhere. At a crossroads a sign read, "This way to heaven; That way to a discussion about heaven". He took the path That way. This preference rubbed off on even the youngest among us. On a Sunday morning during the church service, the wee ones in the Sunday School preschool class were playing in the churchyard when little Amy stood up and announced in her biggest voice, "Everybody make a circle; we're gonna have a 'scussion".

Mark had long since discovered his love of theatre and his gift for writing dialog, and he wrote plays, produced and acted in shows for church and school and joined the community theatre. He generously took Kristi along to auditions when younger actors were needed. His "team sport" in high school was theatre, and in his senior year he wrote and produced a show that earned enough money to pay for the graduates' caps and gowns. It also earned him an award as the most valuable member of his graduating class. Mark accepted his diploma at the Civic Auditorium with lots of Community Theatre friends in attendance, thanking "the Academy and his parents for this honor".

When the youth group decided to host a sock hop in the newly renovated meetinghouse, they invited all the grownups to join in the fun, and circulated a sign-up sheet among themselves for volunteers to bring the food. As the list filled up it became apparent there were no takers to supply salad for an expected overflow crowd, so they came to me in a mild panic, "We're gonna need a bathtub of salad", they said. So...I went to the market and bought a plastic baby's bathtub and filled it with salad! Gotta think like a teenager.

Since we seemed to be drinking coffee with parishioners through much of the day, Irving and I usually had a morning Postum when we got up. Then when June, Mark and Kristi went off to school, we went to our new office, taking Amy with us. About ten o'clock we were ready for some real food, so we'd cross the street and have breakfast at the Greek coffee shop/bus station, or sometimes in the Bangor House. In both places we became friends with the men in charge. Tasos, the hotel's manager and George, the owner of the coffee shop enriched our Bangor experience, and the happy memories of going "out" for breakfast have stayed with us ever since—especially with Amy.

George was, for a time, mayor of the city of Bangor and he had long been a pillar of Bangor's little Greek Orthodox Church. He invited us to be his special guests at the annual Greek folk festival and dinner, where he taught us the steps to the folk dances, and introduced us to all his friends and relations. In spite of the small size of the Greek congregation, this dance was Bangor's biggest social event of the year, with "everybody who was anybody" in attendance, and everyone groaning about tired muscles on the Monday after.

Tasos, the manager of the Bangor house was a handsome New York City expatriate, with a lovely New York girlfriend named Cathie Lamb, and it didn't take long for us to become the best of friends. The Greek chefs of the exclusive hotel restaurant made our Thanksgiving complete the year they, along with Tasos and Cathie, accepted our invitation to share in our American holiday and the Isaksen family traditions. It never occurred to me to worry abut their judging my cooking or to fuss about possible catastrophes. Our heart room needed filling!

Our parsonage had a dining room, which we turned into our at-home office with the partners' desk (a long wood-grain Formica platform on two brown-painted metal filing cabinets) taking up most of the space. Our meals were happily shared in the breakfast room to the rear of the kitchen. The tomfoolery rampant at meals included rivalry for the seat next to Mom and pretend complaints against one another (Irv included) as they stuck out their tongues, made faces, and tattled to Mom "look what he/she is doing!" Laughter reigned.

Little Amy made her contribution from inside a bottom closet of the built-in china cabinet, which she used as a kind of hidey hole and play house. From time to time she would pop out of the closet door and announce, "Don't anybody flush the toilet; I'm gonna take a shower!" I don't remember the water problem indicated, but I sure remember our baby's interpretation of it.

Our Amy loved strawberry jellyroll. It was her special favorite and we were only too happy to give it to her. One afternoon, however, we were amazed to find our little one enjoying her special sweet treat in her own special way. Mark called me into the breakfast room to see her sitting in her high chair, joyfully smearing the strawberry filling and fluffy white topping on her little bare feet.

We also had a sun porch, which may have been the "heart room" of the house, as it welcomed and housed various drop-in and stay-on guests during our years in Bangor. One long-time visitor in particular was Lester, a young musician from NYC who had been on our staff at Rowe camp, and had once sung with Pete Seeger. While he was with us he convinced me to actually sing a solo in church, Judy Collins's "My Father". He stayed longer than we might have preferred but was such a sweet soul, we couldn't imagine asking him to leave. Heart room won the day.

On Thursday evenings we held open house and I regularly made a tall pot of honey-spiced tea to share. Folks from the church dropped in informally with their discussion topics or musical instruments. When one young couple came with their guitars, preparing to play "Amazing Grace," I had the audacity to complain about the words of the classic. They said, "Well, why don't you write new ones?" So I went into the kitchen and did so, immediately. The result found its way into my first book of poetry but as I matured spiritually, I learned to love the real words of the song.

At that time on the east coast the practice of "professional courtesy" gave us, as clergy, free doctor's care and free membership in the YMCA. The beauty of this was Kristi's metamorphosis from a messy little girl into a synchronized swimming goddess who choreographed her own numbers and starred as both soloist and choral member. Somehow coming home with frozen hair never caused her to succumb to winter illnesses and she blossomed in grace and charm.

Throughout the country, women were reading Betty Friedan's *Feminine Mystique* and awakening to their inequality. The Equal Rights Amendment (ERA) was being debated everywhere. I went to Augusta to speak on behalf of the amendment before the Legislature, and was thankful for the radio training I'd received at WCAU when I was a youngster, and for the vocal timbre I'd been gifted at birth. No squeaky, inaudible or high-pitched speeches from this woman!

One afternoon I received a phone call from the office of the Federal District Judge. Scary! What could he possibly want with me? It turned out there was nothing to worry about; the judge was inviting me to offer the invocation at the installation of new federal attorneys and the welcoming of newly naturalized citizens. I wrote a poem inspired by Ecclesiastes and showed it beforehand to a fundamentalist acquaintance, a Pentecostal preacher who worked at the local stationer's. He loved it. I attended the federal celebration and presented my invocation poem. An avowed atheist from our church was among the new federal attorneys that day, and he also loved it. I realized, that day, I am called to be a builder of bridges. With my faith and my writing I can span the distance between.

When we were still in Stafford, my work on DRE Accreditation had put us in the center of the religious education community, and we were invited to train as leaders in the denomination's exciting new curriculum "About Your Sexuality". Offering sex education in the church community was a new and controversial idea, and Irving and I went to Boston to be trained as a teaching team. Amy was not yet a year old, and went with us to the training. The participants declared every conference should include a baby because of the love dynamic she created. The sexuality course was designed for junior high youngsters and was always taught by a male/female team. In each church where the curriculum was to be taught, an introductory course was held for the parents to sample the material, and we discovered that presenters of these sessions should usually be "outsiders" so that the resident clergy and religious educators could minister to and comfort those who became threatened, angered or distressed by the content. In Hartford, CT, the associate minister and the DRE co-led the introductory session and the chaos that resulted nearly got them fired. Irving and I were called in to help calm the troubled waters. In Bangor, however, the adults loved it and decided they wanted to experience the whole course, not just a sampling, so we launched a special "About Your Sexuality" for adults as well as the regular one for the pre-teens. We soon found ourselves on the radio where we were invited to speak in defense of the concept. Shared values taught in a loving community clearly spoke for the family ethic of the liberal church.

Chapter ten
Bronco, boat and toboggan

On the maps Maine seems largely colored blue because of her abundance of lakes and ponds. The difference between a Maine lake and a pond is not based on size, as in the rest of the country, but on the source. In New England a lake is stream fed and a pond is spring fed. Beach Hill Pond is almost three miles long and a mile across, and the winds coming down the pond through the surrounding forest sometimes stir up enormous waves. The breakers roar as they do at the seashore. Vacation cottages, beach homes and lakeside hideaways in Maine are all called "camps", and living in a church-owned parsonage, we decided we needed such a place for ourselves, so we went shopping for a "camp". We found a woodland cottage on Beach Hill Pond, out of Ellsworth, owned by a gay couple from New York. They loved it too much to sell to anyone who might not seem to fit. Fortunately, they fell in love with our family, and were pleased to accept our offer to buy. The place came furnished, and had a fireplace, artesian well, and a screened-in porch.

We owned three "recreation vehicles", a beautiful polished wooden toboggan, a 12-foot yellow Sunflower Sailboat, and a red Ford Bronco that was also our all-purpose family car. We'd pile the kids and a few of their friends into the Bronco and take off for the Lake house, singing "The Cat Came Back", "Charlie and the M T A" or some other beloved nonsense song. Sometimes we played word games like "Botticelli" or "the minister's cat". Once we reached the lake, we'd rig the sails on our little boat and sail the waters of Beach Hill Pond. The first time Kristi saw a Hobie Cat on the lake, with its twin pontoons and raised canvas deck looking like a cot, she cried, "Look, Mom! A water bed!" (This before the arrival of those notorious bedroom monsters gave the term a whole new meaning.)

On one of our trips to the lake house, 3-year-old Amy told me quite seriously, "Mommy, there are two Willies". Was this perhaps a hidden message? The usual response from parents to such a vague comment might be a mindless, "That's nice, dear". It certainly didn't seem to make sense at first hearing. But we asked a few questions about where the Willies were, and what she knew about them. It turned out she had discovered two books at the church by the same children's author and illustrator, (Ezra Jack Keats) telling different stories about the same characters. Too young to have the concepts to describe this interesting phenomenon, she had told me about it the only way it made sense to her—two Willies. Even at so early an age, a child wants to be listened to!

About this time, Irving and I became enamored with the taste of honey. We liked it in our tea and in our coffee, and I played with it in some of my cooking. When we went to the lake house in the summer, inexpensive tomatoes and bell peppers were abundant, and the former owners had left behind some fragrant spices for me to experiment with. I didn't know the name of one delicate powder I especially loved, until I encountered it years later and discovered it was a mild curry. Inventing a simple easy dish to serve with rice I created the family favorite we named Lake House Meatballs, rich with bell peppers, onions, and tomatoes, just a hint of curry and a little honey.

Like their mother before them, Mark and Kristi picked blueberries one summer, but the berries were the low-bush blues that were scooped in berry rakes, not the high bush type grown by True Blue in New Jersey. Mark charmed the old Mainer who supervised the pickers by asking him about himself, showing a true interest that the old gentleman didn't often encounter from a young person. For those of us "from away" it was charming to hear the men of Maine call all the women and children "Deah".

The organist and the choirmaster at the Bangor church were Harold and Bill, an aging gay couple who had been together since their student days at Eastman School of Music in New York state. When the men graduated and moved to Bangor, they applied for teaching space at Harmony House, the music school of renown in the city, and were denied access because of their lifestyle. Anyone in Bangor who really wanted to learn music, however, studied with Bill or Howard in their home. We Unitarian Universalists plotted a sweet revenge, and held a fund raising testimonial concert honoring the two musicians. The results were phenomenal, and we used the money raised to set up a scholarship in both their names—at Harmony House.

When no-fault divorce was approved in Maine, Irving and I became approved marriage counselors under the requirements for couples to undergo counseling in the process of acquiring their decree. Our younger girls understood this to mean we were helping certain people to get "unmarried". Through the good offices of the Maine Pastoral Counseling Association, we in the Bangor clergy were gifted with a workshop "On Death and Dying" with the legendary Elizabeth Kubler-Ross. She was no bigger than a minute, with a soul and intellect as big as all outdoors and the warmest of hugs and smiles. Kubler-Ross totally charmed me and started me on my way to emphasize and cherish grief-work and bereavement counseling in my ministry.

Trips to General Assemblies were always exciting. In our small denomination, we cultivated friendships all across the nation, and loved the "May Meetings" (held in June) where we gathered to learn something new and meet with friends and colleagues. We took Mark out of school to go with us to GA in Boston, and in Toronto, Canada, believing he would learn more in those few days about democracy, debate, Robert's Rules, compassion and fine language, than he could possibly learn at school. I was particularly thrilled at a GA in Boston to meet with Kenneth Patton, the premier poet-liturgist of the denomination. Ken's work dominated the hymnal of the era, and his approval of my own work made me proud.

Irving and I worked as a team doing our pastoral counseling, only rarely seeing clients individually. One couple drove fifty miles from their back-to-the-land farmhouse to church services and counseling sessions for at least a year. The effectiveness of well-planned and themed worship services became apparent to me when Alice, the wife, spoke to me about her aha! moment. Irving and I had been doing that curious tightrope-walking kind of thing ministers and therapists are taught to do—asking the "right" questions, opening up options, teaching communication techniques, and all without advising—encouraging the person to live up to her potential and solve her own problems. In the process, there are some important principals that must be taught, but teaching doesn't really happen until its other half occurs— the learning! And in the wisdom of the great Kahlil Gibran, we're told that learning will happen only when the student is willing to "enter the portals of his own knowing". Well, one Sunday morning it happened. Alice came to me during the coffee hour all excited, and declared that the needed insight had come to her during the service. The music, the readings, the rituals, the sermon had all suddenly jelled for her, and she made her discovery. "That's what you've been telling me for the past year, isn't it?" she asked. Yes Alice—It is!

One of the quiet pastimes that refreshed my spirit at the lake house was putting together jigsaw puzzles. Irv and I were carrying more than a ten-hour a week client load as pastoral counselors in addition to our other ministerial activities and studies, and I found the engagement of both the mental and the physical in puzzle building to be truly restful. We set up our puzzle pieces on an old German indoor picnic table of carved black oak. We'd placed it beneath a window, and when we were not off swimming or sailing, or popping corn and enjoying it on the sofa by the fire, we worked our puzzles by the window, and found serenity.

Among the wonderful people in our Bangor congregation were George Cunningham, a wizened college professor and chess guru who urged me to slow down and speak up when I preached, Jim Henderson, a young family man who ran for state assembly and William S. Cohen, lawyer, politician, athlete and author who was Mayor of Bangor on our arrival. Bill was elected to the U. S. House of Representatives in 1972, Senate in 1978 and appointed Secretary of Defense under Bill Clinton 1997–2001—and I was his minister! Irving and I decided to serve our divers congregation better, we'd each join a different political party. He lost the toss and had to register Republican.

By the time we left Stafford I had completed the required work for DRE Accreditation, and went before the committee in Boston to be awarded my credential, but unfortunately, that wasn't going to happen. During the interview I was asked why I wanted to be a Director of Religious Education. In the process of my studies, I had become aware that I was really training for the parish ministry, and being the bold and outspoken wench I am, I said so. Not a politic thing to do! When the accreditation committee went into closed-door session for their deliberations, the process dragged on and on. Ms. Betty Annastos, a longtime director of religious education and active member of the R. E. Department, was irate. She felt I was disrespectful of her beloved calling and she refused to agree to awarding me certification. The director of the department threatened to walk out if she did not agree, but she held firm. A strong and dedicated woman! Normally a non-award decision would be accompanied with a statement naming the unfilled requirements needed to complete the work and achieve accreditation. Since I had completed all the work satisfactorily, mine did not. So I talked with the Rev. Dr. George Spencer, Director of the Department of Ministry, and garnered a scholarship to enroll in Bangor Theological Seminary, just a block from our Bangor parsonage. As a student once more, I rejoiced!

I had some cause for pride in those years, as one of my poems was chosen to be included in the denomination's Meditation Manual in 1974, and the Humanist Magazine published another in 1975. Perhaps the biggest thrill of all came a few years later, when I was honored with a stanza from my poem, "Credo" quoted on the UUA's beautiful 1984 calendar, along with quotes from Emerson and Channing. A friend asked if my parents had seen the publication and likened it to the A+ papers a mother hangs on the front of the fridge.

Mark, in his junior year won a summer internship with Acadia Repertory Company near Mt. Desert Island. He boarded with an elderly couple who were Unitarians with a son on the faculty of Denison University in Granville, Ohio. In addition to learning professional theatre lore and how to stretch his dollars and find the best bargains when grocery shopping, Mark learned about Denison and its theatre and cinema programs. On returning to high school, he made a filmed audition to apply for acceptance and scholarship. When he left Bangor he became a Denisonian.

A huge heartbreak came for the whole family when our beloved lake house caught fire from a faulty gas heater and burnt to the ground. We lost everything—the cozy German table and benches, my read-to-the-children chaise longue, and an oil painting by my mother of a beautiful Indian chief. Once again, no hysteria. I was just so grateful it hadn't happened when we were in residence, that I refused to cry. I don't think the girls could have been gotten out safely had we been in the house when it caught fire.

Our family auto was now a Toyota wagon, with the license plate UUREVS. As he and I were doing more and more individual work, Irving decided we should have a second car, and he bought a used Volkswagen bug. One of our parishioners, Valerie White, became very active at church and very close to her ministers. She had horses that she invited Irving to ride with her and he began visiting with her frequently. Valerie admired me greatly, and indeed wanted to be me. She came to me for counseling in her rocky marriage, and told me, "Things are so bad with my husband, I have taken a lover". She neglected to tell me it was my husband. I was determined not to be the suspicious jealous wife so when I was faced with the truth the world seemed to come crashing down around my ears.

In addition to my seminary studies, or as part of them, I had enrolled at the Espousal Center in Waltham Massachusetts for Advanced Clinical Training in Transactional Analysis with Dr. Sue Simms Bender. TA was an integrated psychotherapy popularized in the book *I'm OK, You're OK* by Eric Berne. Any therapist studying the discipline also underwent therapy in the process. This course of study was my source of personal insight and support during the death of my marriage.

I had always found it impossible to talk out my fears and concerns with the most important people in my life, beginning with my mother. With Sue's help I went to the root of the problem. When I was born, I needed to be placed in an oxygen tent to aid my breathing, and every winter I would contract a severe case of bronchitis. When I was five the doctor told my mother, in my presence, "She'll have this problem every year until she has a really intense attack that will kill her or cure her". What a message for a child! The winter I was nine, I had a severe case of bronchitis. My dad was working overtime, and my mother had gone to pick him up from work, feeling I was safe in the care of my Uncle Frank. Unkie had worked an odd shift at the police station and had just gone to bed. I woke up having difficulty breathing, and tried to wake my uncle. Not fully awake he reacted in those first moments of much-needed sleep with an annoyed snarl. I began to cry, which made it all that much harder to breathe. I couldn't speak. I was convinced I was going to die; this was surely "the one that would kill her…" The windows and storm windows of the house and those of my parents' car were closed, but when Meme and Papa drove into the driveway they could hear my labored breathing through all that insulation. They charged in and eased my sobs, called the doctor who fed me something black and disgusting, and the bronchitis was finally vanquished. To this day I suffer sympathetic reactions when I'm near anyone with breathing difficulties.

Through the years, my psychological reaction to anger from someone I loved and depended upon for love (Meme, Buz, Irving) would create the same feeling of suffocation, tears and inability to speak. With my husband(s) I would write on a yellow pad the things I felt or feared or was angered by. Anger, however was not really permitted in my psyche—just fear and sadness. In a roll-playing exercise at Waltham, Dr. Sue had me place Unkie in a chair (imaginary of course) and tell him how I felt when I was afraid and he just growled at me. She had me say, "I'm not going to die waiting for you to wake up!" Then she had me put Irving in the chair and say the same thing to him in connection with his moving out of our home to be with Valerie. "I'm not going to die waiting for you to wake up! I found healing in that reassurance that my life was valuable.

The church's reaction to Irving's move was horrendous. A congregational meeting was called with the people planning to accept Irving's resignation and keep me on as minister while I continued seminary and prepared for ordination. I took the mistaken advice of colleagues and did not attend the meeting. Irving, however, did attend, and told those gathered that he was moving back into the parsonage, which he did—very temporarily. The congregation voted to suspend our team ministry, and I was out of a job.

When we looked into getting a divorce we discovered that Irving's previous divorce was not legal. His wife had paid for a swift decree in Alabama, and now learned that the clerk and the judge who had been granting these divorces had pocketed the money without registering the suits. We checked with the Attorney General of Connecticut where we had married and verified that we were legally wed there, because we had had all the official documents. In Maine, however, the judge was not sure whether we should apply for a divorce or an annulment, saying, "If you're not married you can't get a divorce, and if you are married you can't get an annulment". So we applied for both (either/or). The final decision was for annulment, and the papers arrived saying basically, "You are not and have never been married, and you are still married for sixty days". That's the crazy thing called the law.

A delightful fellow who graced our sun porch guest room around that time was Tom Jr. the son of a ministerial colleague Tom MacMullen. Young Tom became great friends with Mark and with typical teenaged whimsy the two of them joined me in what I call the "Trash Bombing" or the "Great Garbage Caper". Winter trash collection was limited to once every two weeks in Bangor, and at the time of Irving's removal to cohabit with Valerie, I was sufficiently distracted to forget to put out the trash on the proper day. No way could that stuff sit around for another two weeks! Woe is me, what to do? Collections hadn't yet been made on the wealthy side of town; why not leave our trash in front of the ritzy houses on the hill? The boys loved the idea, and suggested leaving clues in the bags of garbage indicating that they had been left by Irv and Val. I didn't try that, but we did throw our big plastic bags in the back of Hester the Toyota and drive to the hill, swooping in to bomb the various trash cans along the way with our gift of refuse. Oh how we laughed!

During the painful process of ending the Stevens marriage, my colleagues and advisors in the ministry were most supportive of me and my ministry, and George Spencer, Director of the UUA Department of Ministry promised me a student parish would be found where I could support my family while I continued my seminary work. Unfortunately, Rev. Spencer retired just then and women in ministry were not a priority for his successor, David Pohl. All help ceased.

I knew I had to attend General Assembly that year to find work and make a future for my family. My friend Robert Jordan Ross advised me to apply for a west coast opening with the Service Committee (UUSC) our international volunteer service organization. I had no great desire to cross the continent, but the prospects were good, and Bob told the search committee they would get more than their money's worth if they hired me. They took his advice.

Chapter eleven
California here we come!

Why had two marriages failed? Buz Somers was a good husband. He was what was called in that day a catch—handsome and romantic, from a good family, and going somewhere professionally. He was, however, a literal thinker rather than a lateral (creative) thinker, and he became an accountant. He was not a man of imagination or passion. I loved him, but sadly and inevitably we grew apart.

Irving Andrew was often an angry man, passionate about his liberal beliefs and ready to fight for them and for whatever he believed to be the right thing. He was a caretaker and a taker of risks, and our life was sometimes hectic but it was never boring. He made me laugh. I adored him. Unfortunately, he found it impossible to believe in my love. His childhood with an abusive alcoholic father had scarred him and left him feeling unworthy. When his siblings got into trouble and his father was about to thrash them for some reason, Irving would take the beatings for his brothers or sister. His sense of unworthiness made him take life's beatings as he had taken them for his siblings, and he believed for as long as he knew me that I would someday find someone "more worthy" and leave him.

On my return from a course of study in Chicago, Irving was convinced I had found someone. What I didn't realize until long after was that I had found someone—my separate and sacred self, poet, nurturant woman, playful child, recognized and accepted as an individual, not just half of something as in "DJ-n-Irv". I think my husband believed the only way to prevent my leaving him was to leave first. He told me the woman he chose to leave with was "…a three, and you're a ten; I'm more comfortable with the three". He also told me, "You will never be alone, except by choice". And I have never exactly chosen to be alone, but I have chosen…

How does anyone respond to rejection of her best qualities?

There was nothing I could change, so I found myself no longer a wife, but a single mother, alone for the first time, and venturing out on a trek across the United States. The Service Committee arranged to move me and my family from Bangor, first sending me to Los Angeles to acquaint myself with the area and find suitable housing. My colleague in Canoga Park, Paul L'Herreau, made me welcome and showed me around San Fernando Valley, where I found a comfortable house to rent on Balboa Blvd. near Sherman Way in Van Nuys.

Leaving Bangor was heart-rending. June had decided to stay in the city she loved, and her boyfriend John Cassidy's mother offered her a home with them. Friends had given me love and comfort when Irving left, and our years in the city had built lots of wonderful memories. Because of the long journey and her advanced age, we left our dog Missy with Irv and Val, and planned instead to add a new dog to the family once we were settled in California. My friend Cathie Lamb agreed to go with us to the west coast, and even though she couldn't drive she made the trip much easier by providing adult companionship. Mark had started college a month or so before, and Ohio was on our way, so we stopped off in Granville to see what Denison University looked like and to visit with the young man.

Prior to my call from UUSC I'd had a meeting with a search committee from a church outside Chicago that was considering calling me to be their minister. They were lovely people and I became instant soul-mates with a couple who were members of the committee. Stopping off to visit these new friends on the journey west, we found that their daughter and Amy looked and acted like twin sisters. Our time with them was a high point in our continental crossing.

With me behind the wheel all the way, we passed through Omaha, Nebraska, the city where I was born, and stopped off at the Grand Canyon where Japanese tourists begged Kristi—the quintessential American child—to pose with them for their ever-present cameras. We had giggling fits over my awkwardness at being newly single. While having dinner at a classy restaurant with Cathie, Kristi and Amy, I threatened to hide under the table when some kind gentlemen sent over drinks. Imagine the hilarity that caused! And my discovery out our car windows of strange new birds (magpies!) with erratic flight patterns made me the brunt of new jokes and more teasing. "She thinks she sees zigzag birds!" We should have made the desert portion of our trip after sunset, but in my ignorance, I drove across the Arizona and eastern California deserts in the blazing sun and baked my tires square. Really! Bumping along on square tires is an experience

I never even read about in books! It was a huge relief to reach San Fernando Valley as the sun set so I could stop driving at last. Cathie helped us to settle into our new home, and then back she went to the east coast, soon to leave Bangor and return to her beloved NYC. During the following years we all looked forward to her occasional visits with great delight.

Wherever I live, I know there is beauty to be found or made, and so I made a home in this new land for my family and myself. I made it beautiful in ways I had learned from my mother. That great lady taught me a kind of determination and a "not by bread alone" graciousness which some see as less than strictly rational. Early in my life, Meme taught me the ancient rhyme by James Terry White, about hyacinths to feed the soul. And so I have lived my life and chosen my path, through several decades of genteel poverty, creating a household filled with flowers and laughter and sunshine for the children and other growing things. There are those who have called this foolish.

We had thought about our desire for a canine companion, and decided the dog for us would be a Sheltie, so we found ourselves a miniature "Lassie" and named her Sundance. She was a happy girl as long as we were around to keep her company, but because Shelties had begun to be over-bred, she was annoyingly yappy and drove the neighbors crazy. Luckily my office was in my home so the pup had company much of the time.

My position with UUSC was as co-director of the west coast chapter with Kris Ockershauser. Kris was an experienced community organizer, and with my ministerial background we made a good team. I traveled from church to church across

California, Arizona and Nevada, guest preaching and telling the story of the Service Committee, founded in Europe in the forties to help Jewish intellectuals to escape the Nazis. The philosophy of UUSC was expressed in the proverb, "Give a man a fish and feed him for a day; teach a man to fish and feed him for a lifetime". Projects involved grass-roots participation by the people we were there to help. It was my job to reach out to the more conservative members of our churches who had been alienated during the denomination's struggle toward black empowerment; to show them a broader picture of the worldwide works of our volunteer service organization, and hopefully, to interest supporters in contributing money. One of my first forays into social justice work was a trip into the fields of Ventura County among the farm workers, to better understand the grape and lettuce boycott the local chapter was advocating, and to see firsthand the plight of the immigrant workers. Mark, ever the storyteller, imagined a scenario in which I would be jailed or persecuted in some way, and become a heroine. Nothing dramatic happened.

I was soon invited to the Pacific Southwest District UU Ministers Association gatherings, as one of only two district women in the clergy. The first woman ordained by a denominational body in America was Olympia Brown, ordained by the New York Universalist Convention in 1863. The few women who followed were marginalized in tiny churches and linked congregations with grossly substandard remuneration. By 1975 things were about to change. Today women in the ministry and studying at our seminaries outnumber the men, and many are in the pulpits of large healthy churches across the nation.

My colleagues wondered what church I would choose to attend when I wasn't preaching somewhere myself, and nearby Studio City Church was my logical choice. Jon Dobrer was the minister there, and he became a good friend and a sounding board for my creative thoughts. Our favorite spot was on Ventura Blvd. in Studio City—a little bookstore, gift shop, and luncheon alcove called 'Books Etc.'. There was a balcony at the rear of the shop where we could sit in high-backed wicker chairs and have iced tea and a sandwich while we discussed sermon ideas. Jon would talk about his current topic, and inevitably it resounded with me. There seemed always to be something I had just written in my journal, a poem or pithy piece of some kind to share. He jokingly complained that what I'd written reduced his whole sermon to three stanzas, and I responded, "But I'm the one left in the pulpit with twenty minutes to fill". On Sundays when I was in town, I sat in the second row of the Studio City Church listening to the Rev. Jon Dobrer's brilliant and witty sermons, and bobbing my head in agreement. I accused him of giving me whiplash. Once, in Books Etc. Jon introduced me to Ray Bradbury, as the prettiest minister in California. Not so much of a challenge in those days, with so few of us around. When I chatted with Bradbury and talked about my son and his creative spirit, the great writer said Mark must be like him, an "orange monkey", Ray Bradbury's imagery for the unique and creative among us.

One of the more interesting people I met in the congregation was Suzie, the sexiest gal in Studio City. As a newly single woman, I found Susie's life both intriguing and instructive. Having inherited my mother's full-figured outline, I'd never felt deprived in that area of feminine charms, but with my arrival in California I was suddenly under-endowed—with eyelashes! Susie had a nose that rivaled that of Barbara Streisand and a huge frosted "fro" hairstyle, but she never left the house without her artificial eyelashes, and she was always the darling of an army of male admirers. This didn't quite convince me to try the artificial enhancements, but it was entertaining.

The other two churches in The Valley were Emerson UU Church in Canoga Park, pastored by Paul L'Herreau, and the Sepulveda UU Society in North Hills, led by Farley Wheelwright, a friend and mentor from New England. Farley was the source of one of my best Down East stories (see Pineapple Sage) and had been most supportive in my early days as an aspiring Unitarian Universalist minister. His congregation was housed in an unusual meetinghouse called "The Onion" because of its unique shape. The quaint brown shingled building has strange acoustics that enable anyone sitting on one side of the sanctuary to clearly hear a whispered comment from the other side of the hall.

The folks at Emerson were an actively social group, and I was welcomed at their frequent get-togethers, where we sat in beanbag chairs listening to music, talking and sharing wine and cheese. One of the single men from the group invited me out from time to time, and once made a statement that somehow epitomized male thinking of the era. He said he thought I might like to have a man taking care of my family and me, but the price for that care was, "Don't out-shine me!" For some reason, when I think of this time, I recall the lights on the hills as I drove from place to place. We know that the olfactory sense is the quickest path to memory, and I am exquisitely olfactory, but city lights spark memories for me wherever I see them. I remember those lights on the way to parties at Emerson Church, as I remember them in Philadelphia or Hartford.

My most admired colleague and mentor on the west coast was the Rev. Dr. Stephen H. Fritchman, minister to the First UU Church, Los Angeles. This white haired legend of a preacher had been leading the good fight against oppression during the McCarthy era and before. He had served the Unitarian Church in Bangor from 1932 to 1938, and edited the denominational magazine for years before coming to California. He was a true feminist in a time when there were very few among the men of the nation, and a founding member of the Black Caucus in his LA church and the Black Affairs Council continentally. His birthday was the same day as Kristi's and I was proud and happy for my children to know him, because to visit with the Rev. Steve Fritchman was to be in the presence of greatness. He always treated me like a beloved daughter, advised me wisely, and sent lovely hand-written notes to me on many occasions.

Early on, Bob Kaufmann, minister of Throop Church, Pasadena, kindly encouraged his church board to name me their official marriage minister, which allowed me to marry folks anywhere in California. This was a financial lifesaver during the time before I was called to parish ministry. Among my esteemed colleagues, the game most often played in the male-dominated ministers' association meetings was "mine's bigger than yours", touting church attendance and generally claiming bragging rights in various ecclesiastical arenas. As I sat quietly, listening to the baritone voices vying to outdo each other, one of the men in the group commented on my non-participation. "I've just come from New England", I said, "where I was taught to speak only when what I have to say is an improvement on silence". Embarrassed laughter ensued, and words of admiration and respect.

Kristi had been accustomed to a small student body in her Bangor schools, and suddenly she was attending a junior high school the size of a small college, but she never let the challenge slow her down. By the end of her first year in Van Nuys she presented me with the gavel she won for leadership. Her boyfriend was a cutie named Jim Strauch whom we dubbed "Jim Honey" and his mother, Nancy, a pretty young divorcee who worked as a beautician, became one of my best friends and cohorts. We two had lots of fun exploring the singles scene and imagining our adventures written into a TV sit-com. Our kids once overstayed the town curfew, and got picked up at the local park, swinging on the swings. We had to rescue them from the Van Nuys Police Station where they were treated politely, and with kindness.

My own major dating dilemma was about what to reveal of my profession, and when. If I met an interesting and eligible man, should I invest myself in getting acquainted at some depth only to see him flee as soon as he discovered I was clergy, or should I fess up right away and avoid the disappointment? One place where I was accepted—with "r-e-v" and all—was Valley Ranch, the little restaurant and bar just a half-mile down Sherman Way. In an atmosphere like that of Cheers, I could safely stop in for their delicious BBQ or a glass of wine, and always feel recognized and protected (where everybody knows my name.)

I have been blessed with an exceptionally beautiful relationship with my daughters. Kristi, as a teen, thought me funny and clever, rather than judging me a drag. She wrote exquisite poetry in my honor, and when I quipped and clowned around, she "got it" and laughed. Once she came home with a new gymnastic trick or dance step and asked me, " Mom, would you like to see something really hard?" I responded, "Oh, yes; it's been so long!" and instead of the standard, "Motherrrr!" she giggled along with me. When she thought she had reason to hate me because we were forced to move she had the grace to confine her thoughts to a private diary, revealing the vitriol only into her written sanctuary.

Kristi traveled across the nation with the Spirit of America Chorus, and returned with a developing genius as a writer. I honored that genius with this:

> "What shall I teach my daughters?" I asked myself in an old journal and through the years their lessons have been lived rather than lectured, shared rather than imparted, and we grow ever more alike.

June, my first-born was a little dark-haired beauty who taught me the joys of motherhood, and grew up to be a Carly Simon look-alike. From my mother, and from me, she inherited her delight in flower arranging and her quick appreciative laughter whenever her siblings performed.

Kristi was the next daughter. Such joy to hear this child-woman at fifteen and just returned from an adventure, read from her journal—the shining images, the salty metaphors, the bright new-eyed discoverings of this vast nation seen from a bus stuffed with singing adolescents, or from the stage of a bicentennial fair, a block party, music festival or civic center in some far-off magical city, the top of the Empire State Building, the bottom of the Niagara Falls. She writes with wit, insight, imagination, the gift of poetry upon her lips and guiding her pen.

The youngest of my girls is Amy, and how the little philosopher loved these silly lines:

Dimples on the nose
Dimples on the nose
Amy Jay and Dori Jay
Have dimples on the nose.
This child, too, has grown strong and wise, crafting insight into poetry I share proudly. Amy wrote:
Illness is only an illusion of the mind
Wellness is the reality of the Spirit

Mark came home from college for Christmas holidays and summer break, always carrying a book and various odds and ends on the plane in a paper or plastic bag. In the summer he did yard work to earn money, and rode his bike for miles to accommodate his customers which included acquaintances through Denison U. His visits to California always brightened our lives and increased our eternally abundant laughter. During his off-campus semester, he chose to study in London, the theatre city of the world. While he was there, working in a pizza palace and attending great dramatic productions, a classmate died tragically in her bath. He called home and asked me to send one of my poems to comfort him and his classmates. It was a piece I'd written for a colleague who wondered if his life made any difference in the grand scheme of things. It was called,

"Will It Matter That I Was?"

The girl was quick to smile, but will it matter
That her responses seem to light a room?
Her gift of sunlight made the day seem brighter,
Her laughing eyes dispelled the former gloom.
Our paths converge for what seems but a moment
Viewed in the vastness of the years between
Can such a brief encounter make a difference?
Our lives are touched; what will it finally mean?
Each time another life meets mine, I wonder.
Each time I take the risk of being known
The question comes before me—Will it matter?
Will it matter when my son is grown
That he has been respected, loved and trusted?
That we each see the other as a friend?
That we have taken time for play and laughter,
And argument—with so few hours to spend!
It matters, I am sure—each moment matters.
Each life and each encounter on our way
Will change the world; and we will be immortal
Through all the lives that we have touched each day.

Chapter twelve
Strange lessons

Our next-door neighbor on Balboa Blvd. was Dr. Gloria Bush, founder of MESA Institute. She was an ousted Bernsian renegade who had taken Transactional Analysis "TA" in a new direction. Hers was a process that was totally unacceptable to Dr. Berne. Because she had strayed from Eric's orthodoxy, she had been defrocked or "excommunicated" as a TA therapist. (Or as we say about erring UU clergy—they may not exactly be defrocked, but definitely unsuited.)

Her practice had grown in spite of Dr. Berne, and when she learned of my TA background, she invited me to become co-counselor in her therapy groups. I could learn a lot working with Gloria and her groups, so I gladly accepted.

Dr. Bush had developed what she originally called "Moniker Theory" and later dubbed MESA, Multiple Ego States Analysis (not connected with multiple personality disorder.) MESA was an integrating process that sought to make appropriate use of our various styles of behavior or our different personas. The idea behind Dr. Bush's Moniker Theory was that we could identify certain attitudes, feelings and behavior patterns with our various names and nicknames. Have you ever noticed that the person who looks out at you from your mirror on one occasion may be quite different from the one you see on another? One time perhaps it's Roberta the dignified professional you see; at another it's Bobby the untidy and mischievous kid from the country.

Now there's no problem with having several "ego states", or ways of being you—in fact the healthiest, most secure and centered people usually have quite a few. They just use them appropriately. Here's an example of what I mean by that: My friend Susie in Studio City had a very practical and mundane "self" she called Sooze, who liked to wear an old terry robe and slippers and spend an evening sitting in her rocker, drinking a cup of tea. Sooze was very good at scouring the sink and doing those ordinary homey things that make life run smoothly. Another of Susie's ego states was Stephanie, the glamorous, somewhat helpless, and quite desirable woman who always seemed to have a big entourage of eager men about. When Stephanie was going out on one of her sophisticated dates, it was the practical, capable self— Sooze—who put on the makeup for her glamour gal persona Stephanie. Dr. Bush maintained that the different ego states develop within specific relationships—with parents, siblings, authority figures, friends and lovers—and also within specific life experiences. The therapy part has to do with identifying the damaged ego states and putting them to rest or replacing them with healthy ones, being aware, and getting the various ego states to work together to make your life the best it can be.

Here's an idea of how the moniker idea plays out in my own life. To begin with, I was a happy baby. In fact, Meme and Papa could wake me from a sound sleep and I wouldn't even cry or fuss. I'd laugh and coo and play with them, then peacefully go back to sleep. When guests would come to visit, my folks would wake me up, knowing I'd smile at their friends, and then snuggle back into my crib. And so my mother gave me the moniker "Little Suzy Sunshine". When I was in the parish full time, and members of my congregation dialed my number with some emergency in the wee hours of the morning, it was "Little Suzy Sunshine" they would hear answering the phone with her bright, cheery, "Good morning!" My next moniker was Dossie, Papa's name for his little girl, the Shirley Temple look-alike who memorized poetry and took tap dancing lessons. Later my big sister June's boyfriends called the little scholar "QK", short for Quiz Kid, and June named the blonde teen-age dynamo "Taffy" for her taffy colored curls. There are ego states named Jeanine, the poet, Mrs. O Carter Somers, of the suburban Junior Woman's Club, Gigi, wide-eyed and immensely curious, especially about things sensual and sexy, D.J. Somers, a late-blooming college student, Mom, Dee, Lady, and certainly "Rev" who is an amalgam of several of the others. I'm conscious of calling on Rev. Dori to handle things when the situation calls for professionalism—when I put myself together before conducting worship or hold myself together during a moving speech in a wedding or memorial service. If I'm playing with the kids, it might be anyone from Taffy to QK to Gigi.

After we'd been in California a while, June's situation in Bangor became uncomfortable, and she came out to join us in Van Nuys. She found baby-sitting jobs and sometimes cared for Gloria's fussy dog while we ran our counseling sessions. On one occasion, Gloria told me June had a young man with her in the house, and that was, of course, unacceptable. I left the group meeting and went to Gloria's house to talk with my daughter. "June", I said, "you know your friends are always welcome in our house, but you can't invite anyone to join you while you're baby sitting or puppy sitting in someone else's house. Please tell your friend it's OK to visit you at home, but he has to leave Gloria's now". The friend's name was John Champion Jr. and he was only too happy to come to our house—again and again—though I didn't realize why at the time. When he wasn't riding a motorbike, Johnie drove a low-slung green Pinto, and one night he invited me to ride with him to the beach. On the dark sandy shore near Santa Monica, he kissed me and said, "I love you. I'm sorry!" I didn't understand then why this needed apology, but Johnie's involvement in our lives across the years, with his alcoholism and perpetual drama has made it abundantly clear. Once more life had sent me someone who had a lot to teach me.

Working in cooperation with the UUSC in Los Angeles was a community organizer with the American Friends Service Committee, named Dr. James McGaha. Jim was an elder in the Disciples of Christ Church working for the Quakers. His field of expertise was Constitutional Law, which he taught at various universities, and his passion was prison reform and liberal politics. Jim is perhaps the most articulate man I have ever known, and we became great friends.

Sometime during that first year, Rob, one of the McGahas' sons, ran afoul of the law, and needed a safe haven. Jim and his wife Ruth asked me to shelter their boy for a few days, and the girls and I gladly did so, once more expanding our house room with lots of heart room. My friendship with the McGahas has lasted ever since.

The other friendship that formed through the Service Committee was with a young San Francisco attorney named Ann Grogan. When I traveled to the Bay area for my outreach assignments, she made me welcome in her charming Mission District apartment, and whenever she came to LA she stayed with us in the valley. The children and I came to treasure her friendship and her brilliant and creative mind, and when I was between jobs and desperate for money to keep us housed, she loaned me $500 that I was never able to repay. Ann's other gift to me was a lesson in self-care. Like me, she loved the ocean, and she wisely set aside time to take herself to the sea at least every other month. She knew how to refresh her spirit, and heal her heart.

One of my more memorable UUMA experiences was on the trip to an annual retreat study group called the Refugio Conference. The retreat center was on the coast above Big Sur, and rather than drive and carpool, several of us from LA and Orange County pooled our funds to rent a small plane to be piloted by our colleague Jim Dace. On the way home I rode in the copilot seat, and Jim showed me how to handle the controls. Look, Ma, I'm flying!

I often speak of my Muse, but that is a metaphor for the real source of my poems. I believe they are a product of the cosmos; something Ralph Waldo Emerson called the Oversoul. I am just the conduit for the music that is "out there" waiting to be heard. When UUSC moved me with my children from Maine to California, it was understood the call was to be for a minimum of two years, but at the end of the first year, the funding for the new position was withdrawn. I was jobless and without my extended family, and we needed to move. The move was perhaps a half mile, to a small house on Enadia Way, within walking distance of Amy's school and still in the same school district for Kristi. The loss of my Service Committee employment (the empty purse) was frightening, of course, but I'd survived the heart rending loss of my husband (the empty bed). Then came Christmas and I would not be leading a congregation in celebrating my favorite holiday (the empty pulpit!) I took to my bed with a flu-like illness that put me "out of it" for several days. When I pulled myself together, and returned to my desk, I discovered in my journal, a poem I had written, gleaned from the cosmos while I was isolated with my chills and fever:

Rainbows...
It is time for rainbows.
My eyes have failed to find them in the drought.
Now the rain has come at last,
The sweet refreshing rain
Has washed away the caked and grimy signs
Of dry-rot and decay.
Brown weeds bloom, and green is everywhere,
And I shall go in search of starflowers in the grass.
A dreamer finds stars and diamonds in the strangest places.
A poet hears songs in the throats
Of bullfrogs and lawn mowers.
A madwoman smiles at strangers,
And brings light to the eyes
Of lonely, haunted people.
Praise be to God
For poets...dreamers...fools.

Johnie was a frequent visitor at our house, accepted as a family member, and he decided "DJ" was too androgynous and uninteresting a name for me. "I think your name is really Dori", he said, and everyone agreed. There would be no more automatic assumptions that Rev. D. J. Stevens was a man. And reflecting on Dr. Bush's moniker theory, I liked using Dori, a name for the woman I was becoming, along with my middle name, Jeanine, who was my poet persona.

With Johnie.

I met some strange and interesting people in this new life of mine. One was an artist and writer who created hidden pictures using all straight lines, and wrote about ancient secrets—truths he believed were universally known in ancient times, and hidden from humankind for some obscure reason. His book was never released, and he disappeared, along with his secrets of the universe. A very different individual was a businessman I met who had an auto dealership, and could afford theatre tickets. He took me to see *A Chorus Line*, and hated it as much as I loved it. He was offended and threatened by the homosexuality, and had no idea that the beautiful message of the book was every life is important! One of my favorites! He just didn't get it. It was much more fun going to theatre with Mark, seeing celebrities like Paul Newman in the preview audiences and loving every minute of the vibrant live productions.

I finally found work in West Los Angeles as administrative assistant to Alan L., the president and owner of a small hardware import company. Alan was a sweet-tempered gentle soul who had been a film professional in the days of Senator McCarthy. He carried a huge emotional burden, having chosen to save his family from financial ruin in the fifties by naming names for the black list. My special ministry to him was to teach him self-forgiveness. He was a loving, forgiving person, and if the young man he once was were someone else, he'd have no problem forgiving him. "That young man", I told him, "was indeed someone other than the man sitting here today. Forgive him!" One of Alan's dearest friends and employees was Tricia, a fellow poet and all 'round sister spirit. She wrote and illustrated an epic poem about Nessy, the Loch Ness Monster, and Alan wrote a book praising womanhood and a book of limericks. I was completely in harmony with these dear souls.

Closer to home my life was blessed with another poet friend, Carli Wittenburg, the mother of Amy's classmate, John and his sister Gigi and a member of the Emerson Church. At the height of my personal tragedy in Bangor, I had written a poem called "Exercise in Self-discovery" with a line that says, "I am strawberries and cocoanut", referring to my particular fragrances. Carli wrote a poem about me, saying I was more than that, not easily wilted or crushed, and naming me apple. Ours was a sweet and supportive friendship.

When I was married to Irving, his preference for quiet rather than radio music had put me out of touch with the popular songs and artists of the day, but once more on my own, I began to listen to the soft rock stations and with Kristi, learned what was good on the airwaves. One artist I hadn't yet discovered was introduced to me when someone noticed how much June looked like Carly Simon. I have had a special love for the singer ever since.

Kristi sang with the Spirit of America youth chorus, and toured the country in the summer of '76 and was visited by her grandparents at the Philadelphia venue of the tour. Along the way she noticed how many postcards were either dull and boring, ugly, or "tacky" and she felt bad for the photographers who had shot the bad photos. So she started a campaign of support for the unsellable cards. She initiated a family tradition of sending tacky post cards, which Johnie, her brother and I joined with delight and have carried on ever since. It's amazing, or at least interesting to discover the many tacky candidates available on sales racks across the country.

Although our family had moved to California, we were still carrying forth the struggles we'd begun in Stafford and Bangor—civil rights, feminism, educational openness. During this highly politicized era, it had become questionable in our minds whether or not to even celebrate Mothers Day. It honored a role, after all, rather than the universal gift of parenting or the individual parent. My kids came up with their own solution. One Sunday morning when Mark was home from college, the children mysteriously informed me I must wait in my bedroom until they called me. When they opened my door it was to announce their declaration of this day as "Dori Day". They served me breakfast in bed (really in my preferred armchair) and gave me gifts. Then Mark, the college theatre and cinema major, declared, "Mom, I can't believe you've never seen *Casablanca*. You are culturally deprived! I'm taking you to see it at the Art Cinema tonight".

The custom of declaring Dori Day at their own discretion was my children's great public statement of love, and it continued for many years. One year, they all showed up after a Sunday service in Fullerton and announced to the congregation that I would not be staying for coffee and conversation; they were kidnapping the minister for a celebration of Dori Day. One of my best ever Dori Day gifts was a rattan basket swing which moved from house to house with us and provided hours of comfortable reading space and peaceful rocking. In that pleasant swing, I learned at last how to truly mellow out. Mark has given me some of my most memorable gifts— one a simple white coffee mug with red letters that read, "All this and brains, too!" the other, a greeting card showing a funny little person cavorting in outer space. The message: "The universe is a better place because you're in it". Inside, it read, "A little weirder, maybe, but definitely better!"

One of our family's favorite stories supports our belief that wackiness and weirdness is just plain fun for intelligent persons. When I offer the story, I tell of having a flat tire outside the gates of an old fashioned insane asylum. When taking the wheel from its axel, I place the lug nuts in the hubcap and put it on the road beside me. Then just as I am about to reattach the spare, a car zips past and knocks the hubcap off the road, losing all four nuts. I'm horrified and frantic, because, obviously, I cannot reattach the wheel. As I stand wringing my hands, a face peers through the locked gates of the asylum and the fellow beckons me over. "I see you've got a problem", he says. "Here's what you need to do. Take one nut from each of the other wheels and attach that spare tire with the three nuts. All four tires will be a little less safe, but it will get you down the street to the garage, where you can get lug-nuts for all the tires. Not perfect, but it'll work". Wow!" I say, "That's amazing. That's brilliant! What are you doing locked up in this place?" "I'll have you know, Madam", he retorts, "I'm crazy, not stupid". So are we all in our family; delightfully "crazy" but never stupid.

When Alan's hardware business took a downturn, he regretfully gave up my services, and I looked for work elsewhere. I found a writing job with a *Playbill* type magazine out of West Hollywood, and for a short while enjoyed an exciting career change. I interviewed the legendary designer, Edith Head, and covered the filming of *Circus of the Stars*. At the grand opening of L'Hermatage Hotel, I attended the rooftop reception where I met Cary Grant and other luminaries. This all seemed too good to be true, and perhaps it was, because one day when we on the magazine staff went to work we found the two young publishers had disappeared, taking our work and our paychecks with them. The loss of my written work was even more devastating than the loss of my salary, because it deprived me of material that would have greatly enhanced a writing resume.

Back in the valley, Kristi graduated from Junior High School and sang "Yesterday" at the ceremony. She made me immensely proud, as always. About this time the Unitarian Universalist congregation in Fullerton began negotiations with me to become their part-time minister. They had a "futures fund" of $500, and knew they needed professional leadership to have any future at all. I traveled to Fullerton planning to help them for a couple of months, and stayed on as their minister for nearly ten years.

Chapter thirteen
Many jobs, one calling

As I review my life's journey, I begin to understand what life demands of me. I've learned it's up to me to keep moving ahead and continuing to grow in ministry. I have been blessed with such wonderful children, bright and beautiful, wise and kind. They teach me so much, and always make the journey worthwhile. So— let it be a dance!

My commuting from San Fernando Valley was not working. One family in the church offered the use of a room in their home for an office, but that proved to be unworkable. As soon as we were on our way as a congregation, I negotiated with the Methodist Church for the rental of their second parsonage on the corner of Fullerton's Lincoln Ave. and Dorothy Lane. I needed to be in the community I was to serve. This, of course, meant moving the girls to new schools. Kristi was about to enter High School and she somehow overcame her hatred of the move (and of me for being its cause) and once again became a leader in her class. Amy was fortunately enrolled in the forward-looking Acacia Elementary School's gifted program, and June tried Fullerton Junior College.

I had a little wall plaque in my study with which I identified very strongly. It was a drawing of a funny little lady with wavy hair, standing in her bathtub and peering out from behind her shower curtain, surrounded by plants. She was sharing her space and the rich moist atmosphere of her bath with all her green and growing friends. The caption read, "How's your fern?" Nurturing and caring for my houseplants or the geraniums, herbs, and begonias in a tiny patio garden is one of the best ways I can get the TLC I need for myself. It's that old truism, "givers gain" and by caring for the plants, I give myself a gift of life and love, I create serenity and nourish my spirit. In short, the plants take care of me.

The Fullerton congregation met in the auditorium of the Fullerton Museum, and early on I spoke of the need for intellectual, emotional, aesthetic and inspirational elements in the Sunday services. In response to the part about aesthetics, one of the members of the church appeared the following week with two beautiful plants and plant stands to enliven the somewhat austere room in which we met. The plants came to live with me and traveled back and forth between our home and the museum in Hester, our Toyota wagon. We in the ministry call this movable feast "church in a box". Shortly after this routine started, a man in the congregation produced a cartoon sketch for the church newsletter. It was once again a funny little curly-haired lady, this time waving from the front window of her station wagon. On the roof and hood and in the windows were fronds and leaves and potted plants. The caption read: Sister Love's Travelin' Church and Plant show.

Well, now you know one more thing about me—I'm a plant freak. I call myself a cardaholic as well, because I can't resist a clever greeting card. I have even been labeled a "visionary" by one of the faithful but she wasn't at all sure that was a complement. She may have meant I was somewhat less than accurate in my perceptions of reality—a dreamer, a space cadet, a flake. However, the scientific reality is this: the subconscious and the super-conscious speak only the language of pictures—visions, imagery, dreams, insights. To visualize is the beginning of creation. To be a visionary is to see with the mind's eye the possibilities, the potentialities, the plans and blueprints of what might be. To be a dreamer is to be a prophet. Would that I had found a hundred souls to share my vision.

The Fullerton Installation and Ordination Service was like a wedding day, with lots of friends and colleagues there to celebrate me. The lovely folks at First Methodist let us use their large sanctuary, and we held a Champaign reception at the museum. Jon Dobrer delivered the sermon, and Kristi sang "What I Did for Love" The great Stephen Fritchman gave the "Charge to the minister". He was my hero; and he charged me to be "...a pioneer of a new age, a minister to the people, a woman, a friend, a prophet, a poet, a priest." He was using the concept of prophecy, not as foretelling, but as telling forth—speaking my truth, that which needs to be spoken. My truth is: "We are co-creators of our own reality; so choose joy".

As we settled into life in Fullerton I decided to abandon the use of Irving Stevens's name. When he left it seemed to me he took his name with him (along with his vasectomy). Although they had always shared my current name, Kristi, Mark and June were born Somers, so Amy and I reclaimed the Somers name and all of us were known henceforth as the Somers family.

Some very special people came into our lives in Fullerton. Birdie and Charlie Reed, owners of Brewer's Stationers, had once been members of the UU congregation in Whittier, but Charlie, an ardent pacifist who looked like a Marine Colonel, wasn't overly fond of clergy. Over the course of a few months and lots of visits to their shop, I won Charlie over and in the process, became his little sister and his minister. He sometimes introduces himself as my son's and daughters' uncle, and the Reed's daughter Carolyn calls me "Mom". Charlie and Birdie became my dearest friends and faithful members of the Fullerton church for as long as I was the minister there.

The arrival in town of Marj and John Wyckoff changed the fortunes of the church and brought me into the computer age. The cost of renting space at the Museum while paying for part-time professional leadership had become prohibitive for our tiny congregation so we moved the Sunday service into the parsonage living room. That was when John and Marj first found us, and they quickly became loyal supporters. As a successful business man, John guided us toward financial responsibility, Marj became church treasurer and began sending out regular pledge statements, and the two of them pledged matching funds to round out a workable budget. John encouraged me to trust my own strengths and to speak out the truth as I saw it. "What do *you* think?" he would say.

As the designer and editor of our church newsletter, I used the current methods of the day—cut and paste, rubber stamps, freehand drawings. The Wyckoffs offered to let me use the Fitch Wyckoff Company computer, a huge $10,000 mainframe, to put together church copy and John began teaching me how to use a mainframe computer. A Sean

Connery type "A" personality who had founded his own motorcycle aftermarket company, John traveled around the country visiting cycle shops and teaching the store owners how to grow their businesses. He coined the name Hein Ghericka as a motorcycle leathers designer for Harley Davidson, and had the leathers manufactured in Hong Kong. Marj was the company comptroller.

One morning I got an urgent call from Marj asking me to come to their office. John had just left on a continental jaunt, Marj was due to fly out to the manufacturers in Hong Kong, their partner was an unreliable alcoholic, and their office manager had just had a mental breakdown and quit. Would I please fill in for her at the office and keep an eye on things while both of them were away? Ministry sometimes takes strange forms. I worked at the Fitch Wyckoff office for a week or so, talking regularly with John by phone to supplement the computer's instruction manual and do what needed to be done. I learned more than I could have imagined and entered fully into the age of technology, the computer age.

Kristi's friend Danny Glickman from the valley had taken me to my first rock concert, to see Rod Stewart, the quintessential Rock Star. He'd planned to take Kristi, and when she was unable to go with him, he took Mom instead. Danny organized his own rock band, and when he offered to play for us in Fullerton we said yes. We canvassed the neighbors and invited them to join us, then held a Rock Concert in our Methodist parsonage home. Thespians and musicians from the High School jammed the place, and everyone had a wonderful time.

Another of Kristi's friends from the valley was Anne Davis, whom she knew from Spirit of America chorus. Anne's family was Jewish, but her folks generously let us "borrow" their sweet girl to be part of our family—especially at Christmas every year. She sang with Kristi at our Christmas Eve services and donned the Santa hat to take her turn handing out presents and opening stockings along with the rest of us. When Anne's mother died, her family turned to me to conduct her memorial, and when Anne married, I officiated once again, part clergy, part mother of the bride.

In July 1979, my parents celebrated their sixtieth wedding anniversary, and June and Bud, who were about to celebrate their thirtieth, threw a huge party with renewal of vows and an immense guest list that included even distant cousins and long lost friends. I could not have found the money to fly back to New Jersey so was not included. I knew there was enough in the Dietrick purse to send for me if they chose to do so and I felt deeply hurt to be left out.

The Fullerton Methodist minister's daughter, Debby Kennedy, was among Amy's good friends, and his wife Joan became a pal of mine. She spoke of my always looking professional and "put together" even in casual clothes, and I assured her that was exactly what I did, I put-myself-together. Hmmmm. Sometimes that isn't easy. When an associate minister was interviewed for First Methodist, their church board decided they might need their number two parsonage, so they asked me to find somewhere else to live. Determined to keep Amy in her beloved Acacia School, I found a house about four blocks away on Cornell Ave. and we moved.

On the day after moving day my parents arrived for a visit. I was scheduled that afternoon to conduct a memorial service for a young mountain man who had come to the church for a short time, and had committed suicide. With all this drama, Meme and Papa got a small idea for the first time of what it means to be a minister and a single parent. My mother, who once criticized me for wanting her approval, gave me the most accepting and complementary evaluation she had ever given me, saying, "Your children have turned out wonderfully; I could never have done what you have done—alone!" While they were visiting, Papa decided to help Amy get settled into her new room. Much to his amusement, she told him about sorting her stuff and getting rid of the excess. Remembering her mom's words—she'd been asked to be "brutal" in clearing out anything she didn't use, so she told him, "I've gotta be mean"—her interpretation of brutal tidiness.

Kristi's dearest friend in High School was Ernie Kelsey, and his buddy Pat Patterson was like a brother to him, having been his pal since childhood. Pat and Ernie didn't quite live with us, but they were definitely family. One morning very early I had a call from Ernie, telling me Pat's brother had committed suicide, and asking if he should bring Pat over. "Of course!" I said. I did grief work with Pat, then with his mother and sister, and with his estranged father. We worked through bereavement counseling, and preparing a service to celebrate a life too soon ended, while building bridges for family unity. Some months later I was able to celebrate Pat's sister's wedding and share in the family's happy moments as well.

Members of the clergy know that there are no part-time ministries, only part-time remunerations. With a family to

124

support, I have found it necessary to do what amounts to two concurrent full-time jobs during most of my years in the ministry. While in Fullerton I managed a little dance studio, Bailey's Young World, in Cypress. One of the perks of that job was free dance lessons for Amy. I laughed about my beautiful little WASP child seeming to disappear amid the array of blonde youngsters clad in black leotards, while I had no trouble at all in finding my Asian, Black or Hispanic girls. All those little white kids looked alike!

I worked at an advertising agency for a while, hoping to be allowed to write advertising or make use of my art skills, but that did not transpire. Only the male employees became account executives, and I was kept busy typing, which I have always done rather badly, and carrying out various mindless and boring procedures. My gifts were totally wasted. The job that finally made use of my skills was as editor of the Orange County Business Letter, where I encountered another large computer mainframe. I wrote and edited that paper for the length of its publication life.

Our sister congregation (or perhaps mother congregation would be more accurate) was the Anaheim fellowship, a strongly humanistic activist group, called by some a Marxist cell, and led by the brilliant poet, Maurice Ogden. The Fullerton group had split off from Anaheim some years before, and Maurice befriended me when I came to town, coming to my rescue several times, when my car broke down on the freeway, or I ran out of gas. Maurice was great at coming up with words I "lost" when writing a sermon or simply expressing myself for fun. What happens to lost words, anyway? Do they hide in some other dimension and make up stories about us in this one?

My friend Jim McGaha met with me for lunch from time to time, allowing me to bounce sermon ideas off him with his fine mind. The dear man always called me "Gorgeous", and he provided spiritual sustenance and intellectual stimulation whenever I needed it. When Jim and Ruth left California they left sadness in my heart and a big hole in my intellectual life. Before he left, however, Dr. McGaha nominated me to the Board of Centerforce, an organization which provided a support system for visiting families of California state prison inmates. Those who were visited regularly by their wives and families had a greatly reduced rate of recidivism, so we provided a stop-off place for visitors to rest and find a snack, borrow appropriate clothing when needed, and to find help with the small children. I also served on the board of the Women's Transitional Living Center (WTLC) the first and largest shelter for battered women and their children in the state, located in Fullerton. The church took the shelter on as their social action project, and we held fundraisers, collected clothing and supplies for them, and painted and refurnished rooms in the house.

I was elected vice president of the District UU Ministers Association, and enjoyed arranging for the annual getaway to Palm Desert, when the ministers and their significant others spent a few days together—ate, drank and were merry, attended workshops, listened to a colleague's spiritual odyssey, and on the final night always went dancing! As the ratio of women in the UUMA increased, so did the seriousness of our times together. When a man does something—right or wrong—the man is judged by his action; when a woman does something, all women are judged by her action. These new female clergy dared not be frivolous! So the dancing and hilarity stopped and with it, a needed aspect of our spiritual renewal. I missed the fun times with the good old boys, even if they spoke when silence might have been better.

Though we moved a number of times, each of our homes in Fullerton was known by the same name: "Dori's Dorm". Most Saturday mornings found my living room floor littered with teens in sleeping bags. The dogs loved this almost as much as I did. On Cornell we'd inherited Johnie's dobie mix, Prince, the most loving of dogs, who had ridden with his human on a motorcycle, wearing earphones and listening to rock and roll. Poor Prince went into a panic at the sound of thunder or fireworks but trusted me to protect him from the big bad noise as he protected me from all else. He also feared the vet, so in his final days, we kept him comfortable at home rather than tortured with fear of the dreaded animal doctor. When Prince died, Charlie Reed came to my aid, and helped me take him to his final rest at the county shelter. These animal friends are not pets to own, but companions to respect.

The girls who hung out at our house spoke of my bedroom in hushed voices as "the room" and when in need of spiritual sustenance, that was the place they wanted to be, the ambience bringing them peace and comfort. Except when Kristi surprised me with her friendly freaky Muppet, "Animal!" I would walk into my room to find Animal! Staring out from my closet, hiding behind the bed pillows or hanging around in the bathroom. It was always good for a laugh!

At some point, Junie missed her life in Maine, and she returned to the Cassidy's home in Bangor. She began working as a nanny for a former classmate's troubled boys, and in effect raised two mentally challenged youngsters, while their mother went out to work as a nurse. Living in a Catholic household, June found her spiritual home at the Bangor Universalist Church, and an extended family when she sang with the Bangor Chorus. She kept us posted with newsy letters and was religiously faithful about sending birthday and holiday greeting cards and gracious thank you notes.

When Amy was perhaps ten or twelve years old, Kristi was teaching her UU church school class, and asked the youngsters to complete the sentence, "No kid of mine will ever have to blank. Kristi expected something like, clean up their room, or go to bed before 10 o'clock. However Amy wrote, "lie to me". No kid of mine will ever have to lie to me. Why do we sometimes feel we have to lie to a parent, authority figure or partner? We lie to protect the self, or the relationship, to keep from losing love or support. If I know you accept me totally, however, I can confess my shortcomings, failures, mistakes, "sins". I can tell you I've broken your favorite crystal goblet, or attended a fundamentalist church, or bought something of which you might not approve. I know you will separate who I am from what I have done or failed to do, and you will continue to treasure me and respect me anyway. To my own parents, I gave access to only a part of the "truth" of who I am. They didn't want to know what I believed, what I defended, with whom I associated. They did not appreciate my lack of prejudice in surrounding myself with interesting people without considering their "category". They didn't want to hear that certain words and labels are unacceptable to me.

Chapter fourteen
Coming of age

A group of women in Orange County had been together in a business management class at UC Irvine's evening school, and bonded so tightly they refused to stop meeting at the end of their course. They formed an organization of female business and professional leaders and named themselves "Women in Management". Monthly dinner meetings showcased motivational speakers and offered opportunities for networking (the big buzzword at that time, in the business and professional world.) I joined the group and eventually served as third then first vice president. WIM became part of my continuing education.

As I was exploring Fullerton one day, I noticed a shop with an interesting name, The Erogenous Zone. With my insatiable curiosity I had to check it out, and I met the owners, Carla and Bob Souter. It was a combination "Head Shop" and sex toys and lingerie store, and I recognized Carla immediately as a soul-mate. When I'd first arrived in California, I was bemused and confused by the little stores I saw that were identified as head shops. What could that mean? Hair stylists? Hats? Wigs, perhaps? It turned out to mean recreational drug paraphernalia—bongs, marijuana papers, roach clips, incense, psychedelic posters, tie-dyed T shirts. The Erogenous Zone was a magnet for some of the most creative and witty people in town. Immediately after graduating from college Mark had gone to Seattle to live, and when he decided to rejoin the family in Fullerton, he found work at "the Zone". He worked with Tobin, who was an artist, and with Sharon Soderman and Gail Marshall, both of whom became my life-long friends. At some point, I bought a feathered roach clip that was quite pretty. That clip became a delicious little inside joke, because I used it to decorate the top of our Christmas tree, as a kind of psychedelic angel.

Among the people we met at the Zone were Dr. Michael Riskin and his wife, Anita Banker who taught sexuality classes at their Riskin-Banker Psychotherapy Center. They thought it would be mutually beneficial for them and for me as clergy, if I would attend one of their workshops. In that class I learned a valuable lesson. Anxiety cannot exist in the present moment. During an exercise called sensate focus, we were to concentrate fully on the here and now experience of touching, hand to hand, and it became clear that anxiety is, by definition, not about the now, but about what has already happened or what may be going to happen. One more lesson—be here now.

Ric Masten, the Unitarian Universalist troubadour minister, and his wife, Billy Barbara, had come to Bangor to present a poetry concert when we were serving the church there. They stayed with us in our home and over the years, became good friends. For decades, Ric's writings have entertained and inspired Unitarian Universalists all across the continent, and my baby girl had her first taste of poetry as a gift from this wise and wonderful artist. She even today rattles off her first memorized verse, *the homesick snail by ric masten*. When the Mastens came to Southern California on tour, they gave a concert in Fullerton, and once more stayed with us. Ric remembered my poetry, so different from his own, and asked that I gather my poems together so that he could publish a collection of my work. I began to do just that, and in the process wrote the title poem of my first book, *Weeds? Or Wildflowers!*, quoting Ric I wrote: "You're a romantic, my friend said…" And as the work progressed, Ric recalled that like himself, I had a background in art, and he suggested I self-publish. He told me how to go about the process and Marj Wyckoff, my book's "angel" provided the money for the printing.

While in Fullerton, I served on the Boards of deBenneville Pines, PSWD, and Sunset Hall, our progressive Los Angeles retirement home. It seemed to me that I suffered a period of burnout every May, when I'd begin to question my sanity at dedicating my life to ministry. One summer I refreshed myself by reading every Agatha Christie mystery in the local library. I've been a mystery addict ever since. The church eventually outgrew my living room, and I arranged for the free use of the community room at Fullerton Savings Bank, where we once again produced "church in a box".

My friends, the Riskins, had a daughter the same age as Amy, and because they were no longer actively pursuing their birthright religion of Judaism there would be no Bat Mitzvah for Laura. To make up for that loss, they asked me to conduct a coming-of-age class for girls in the Unitarian Universalist church, and I did so with great pleasure. Amy invited Beth and Jessie Kohler, some friends from school to join the class and I explored with the girls their spiritual, philosophical, ethical and religious questions and understandings. We met regularly for eight months, and we explored some old and some new questions. We kept a journal.

When they first met with me, these young women made lists of the things they loved to do; and we noted how many of the things on each of their lists they did alone, how many with other people. Surprisingly, perhaps, most of the things on the lists didn't cost any money and lots of the things on the lists, they thought might be on lists made by their Moms or Dads. They talked about what was important to them, what made them happy, or angry, or sad, what they were worried or frightened by, and what made them proud. They decided it was pretty likely that a good part of their value systems came from their parents, their families, teachers and friends.

They realized too that we all have support systems that have helped us to become the people we are. There are doctors for health and parents who give us self-confidence by saying out loud the good stuff about us. They listed as parts of their support systems: the sanctuary of my room; the teacher who said it's OK to admit you don't know and the one who taught independence, dependability and stick-to-itiveness; the teacher who taught them to dare to be different enhanced their self-esteem and promoted creative thinking.

There were those things our girls had actually inherited from their families—mom's nose, dad's eyes, Grandpa's "greasepaint in the blood" or brother's kindness, answered with kindness. A lot of our understanding of what is important comes from our families. In our journal we wrote about interacting with others in a positive way and in great big letters: L-O-V-E! The list of what's important includes hugs and play, and practical things like food, shelter, clothing and transportation. It includes ways of being that these young women found important—like not sitting in judgment of others, listening to advice but making our own decisions, settling arguments by negotiating, losing gracefully, and winning gracefully, being generous. They included on their list of important things: nature, time with people but also time alone, family sharing, laughter, openness and conversation, combining honesty with kindness, and hugs. Touch is important.

One vital thing this group learned is that it's OK to be proud of life well lived. Not hubris or overweening pride that makes us feel better than... but the healthy pride in who we are and how we behave that allows us to be productive and compassionate humans. We found an article on pride that week in the *Orange County Register*. It's funny how the right thing seems to come along at just the right time. We had a "brag session" at the beginning of each meeting of the group, and some of the things the girls said they were proud of included being able to choose friends without regard for race, not losing my temper but punching a pillow instead, speaking up for what I know is right, overcoming bad habits— and for one young woman, being a birthright Universalist Unitarian.

"We have a pretty terrific history of people I'd like to know!" she said. And this became one of the games we played— naming people living or dead whom we would like to talk with personally. The list included great-great-grandparents and ancestors, heroes like Abraham Lincoln, Jesus or even one of his contemporaries, Martin Luther King, John or Robert Kennedy, Mark Twain, and Eleanor Roosevelt. And they wanted to talk with some of the great Unitarians and

Universalists like Ralph Waldo Emerson, Henry David Thoreau, Elizabeth Cady Stanton and Susan B. Anthony.

They also wanted to talk with some of the people who were bad for the world—like Jerry Falwell or Hitler—to see if they could somehow set them straight. Ah the confidence of youth!

Another way the girls looked at what is important was by exploring what made them angry. In most of our stories the anger was caused by dishonesty, when a friend lied or misled us, and especially when parents didn't have enough faith in us to tell us the truth. There were lots of strong feelings about that. A simple list of what makes us angry placed having someone lie to us first, and it included broken commitments, unkind treatment, unfairness, injustice, rudeness, being ignored or put down, and some of those frustrating things we have no control over. What makes us happy is kindness, attention, being able to give someone something, do something for them or teach them something. Accomplishment makes us happy, and seeing others happy does, too. Nature, a nice day for a walk or a ride in the countryside, and good news makes us happy.

Friendship—now there's something to talk about. To have friends, you need to be satisfied with yourself as a friend to both yourself and others. Pretty wise coming from a group of adolescent girls, isn't it? They also said they like to learn from their friends, to be able to trust and admire a friend—trust is vital to friendship, along with openness, common interests, humor and love. The qualities we look for in a friend are usually qualities we want to develop in ourselves—honesty, dependability, loyalty, trustworthiness, discretion, respect, intelligence, courage, humor and love! As always, the young ones had a lot to teach me.

Chapter fifteen
Marba and music

Kristi was in Fullerton High class of 80, and when we discovered I had no school colors—nothing red—to wear to a ball game she loaned me her red football jersey with "80" and her nickname, "Bubbles" on it in white. She and the gang decided I was so short I must be Bubbles Junior. My vertically challenged stature has been a source of family jokes ever since my stately children achieved their first inches of height superiority. Unable to reach some plate or packaged goods, I would stand in the kitchen and call out, "I need a tall person!" I still do, but living alone, there's no tall folks to be had.

When in her senior year, Kristi auditioned for a dinner theatre production of *Grease*, and got the role. The show's opening date conflicted with Fullerton's graduation, so she "walked" with the Rydell Ringtails, instead of the Fullerton graduating class. Our starlet was on her way! Kristi worked between acting calls delivering singing telegrams. Her assignments took her to Hollywood to surprise Gene Kelly and other prominent personages. As her birthday approached, she confided her wish for a surprise party of her own. Some challenge! I set it up with her employers to send her on a fake assignment at a downtown restaurant, where her family and friends had gathered. When she came to deliver her song, we surprised her with a Humphrey Bogart messenger proclaiming her birthday, and the gathering of all her loved ones. I pulled it off! And she was actually surprised.

She earned her SAG card in the movie *Rumblefish*, directed by Francis Ford Coppola. We moved from the house on Cornell to one on Yale, two blocks away. This one had a swimming pool. Our dog, who identified himself as Kristi's pet, was a shepherd she named Beau. This charmer loved to fetch, and especially loved it when we'd drop a stone in the deep end of the pool, so he could dive down 12 feet and recover it. When we failed to play his game, he'd drop the stone himself and dive in after it. On the day of our move we had a few moments of panic when Amy couldn't be found. She turned up in her new bedroom, buried beneath a pile of throw pillows, sound asleep after the exhausting efforts of the move. Church folk had helped with the process, and when they left in the afternoon Mark insisted I rest, too, and we all went for a swim.

While we were in the Yale Street house, Kristi landed a role in a movie that was filming in Las Vegas, and Beau missed her so much he escaped the fenced-in yard and set out to find her. We never saw him again, and we all grieved for our beautiful funny diving dog.

Pat and Ernie continued to be part of our household with their frequent visits and merry antics. If the photos and paintings on my walls were suddenly hanging upside-down, I knew the boys had been at work. And with a nod to the beach boys, they could be seen scooting down my halls on a sliding rug, singing about throw-ruggin' USA. Along with Kristi, the boys decided that the eggplant has been misnamed. It neither looks like nor tastes like eggs, and is far too beautiful a vegetable, in its purple glory, to be so-named. They re-named eggplant "Marba" honoring its marvelousness. My friend Ann Grogan had given me a recipe for a wonderful dish using eggplant, mushrooms, sherry and cheese, which we gloriously titled "Marba Casserole". It was a favorite for years!

In the early eighties the great psychologist and author, Rollo May had just completed his keynote address before the PSWD district assembly. He had fashioned his remarks around his recent best seller, *Freedom and Destiny*, and began the Q & A portion of the program. After several unremarkable questions and answers, the Rev. Brandy Lovely, a well-known theological intellectual, stood up and asked him, "What about Grace?" challenging the honored guest to defend his position in the religious arena. Rollo May stood quietly pondering for a moment, until this intrepid young clergywoman raised her hand. The big man recognized me and invited comment. "Dr. May", I said, "I've come to believe that the gift of Grace is a sense of humor". "Ah", the unpretentious and gracious gentleman responded. "I wish I'd said that!"

Amy's dearest friend and adopted "sister" was Shannon Bartles who, being graced with a beautiful voice, sang with her at Christmas Eve services just as Anne Davis had sung with Kristi. Shannon was one more beloved daughter, and when she was ready to marry her childhood sweetheart Eric Bauserman, she brought him to me to discuss the wedding. Eric, like my big brother Charlie Reed, didn't like clergy very much, so it was a great joy to be lovingly accepted into his life and to be dubbed "Mom" by him as well as Shannon.

The fourth Fullerton house we lived in was a fixer-upper on Kroeger, close to the original Methodist parsonage homestead. It belonged to a member of the church. We did a lot of cleaning, gardening and clearing out here, and welcomed the kids from yet another theatre department as Amy grew into her immense talent and professionalism. We could never be without a dog for long, so we adopted another black shepherd mix. He regaled us by gobbling up insects, and Mark named him for the bug repellant, Black Flag, called Flag, for short.

One Saturday afternoon, I was driving our ancient Volkswagen bus on Pacific Coast Highway on my way to officiate at a wedding at Crystal Cove State Park when I missed seeing a car in my rear-view blind spot and was broadsided, ending up in Hoag Memorial's intensive care unit. I'm told I remained conscious long enough to inform the rescuing officers they had to tell the bride and groom what had happened and find a minister to conduct the wedding on the beach that I was about to miss. One of the park rangers sped to Laguna Beach, found a clergyman and transported him by Jeep along the beach to perform the marriage. Mark was the one who got notification of my accident, and my friend Carla drove him to the hospital, where they found I was bruised and battered, and my back was in bad shape, but I was going to be OK.

Carla and Bob were no longer married and she eventually became a roommate at the Kroeger house. The whole family loved having her with us, with her ready smile and sweet disposition. She and I were so simpatico and in harmony we joked about getting married. Sadly her situation changed all too soon and she moved to her new home after only a short stay.

In the summer of 1985 my Papa had a stroke and was hospitalized. I desperately wanted to go back east to see him, but I couldn't find the money to pay the fare. The General Assembly of the UUA was being held in Atlanta that year, and of course I wouldn't be going there, either. John and Marj Wyckoff decided I must go to GA, and I should go by way of New Jersey so that I could bid my father farewell. They paid for my trip. When I visited his hospital room, Papa told me about going to choir practice as a boy with the orphans' choir at an Episcopal church in New York City. He said his path led past the Unitarian church. "There were a lot of presidents of the United States who were Unitarians", he said. It was his way of recognizing the legitimacy of my ministry. He died at age 89 and I wrote in the church newsletter:

Papa

Papa has died… slipping quietly from this existence on the sweetness of my mother's kiss, after a 66-year marriage filled with life lived zestfully, lovingly. The long hard summer behind us, we weep at our loss and celebrate our priceless legacy. Papa is dead, we say, and yet within our hearts we carry his life entwined with ours, and he lives in the myriad beauties he has taught us. Charles Arthur Isaksen, his 89 years spanning the twentieth century, knew how to be gentle before other men had learned the strength of gentleness. He was a "feminist without portfolio" by reason of his true respect and love for his wife and daughters. In a time and culture that valued sons more highly than daughters, he smiled a secret smile, claiming Grace because God had given him girls. He demonstrated to us all, before the "experts" discovered it, that anger was wasted energy if vented on another human being.

"I'm not mad at you, Babe", he would say. Although he used traditional Christian language, his talks with me about religion were in harmony with my Universalism, his awe the father of my own spirituality. Craftsman, carpenter, actor, wild-flower gardener, lover of song, warm host to all—this was the ever-smiling man who danced with me in his arms before I learned to walk, the man whose love of theatre graces the souls of his grandchildren and great-grandchildren. Papa dead? Never! He lives on in me and in my children and their children, in all that I teach, and in those who listen, in all who knew and loved him. How fortunate we are.

As a member of the deBenneville Pines board, I set out to write a mission statement for our camp and conference center, with the help of a colleague, the Rev. Dennis Daniel. Our collaboration blossomed into simpatico and affection. Dennis was in the process of ending his marriage to a Unitarian woman active in the Long Beach church, and his children were struggling with some heavy emotional baggage. Their mother had committed suicide some years before, and they were sorely troubled. Dennis and I fell in love, and planned to marry. He moved into our Kroeger Street house with his nine-year-old son and fourteen-year-old daughter. For the first time, the heart room/house room formula did not hold. The situation with the two children was too grim, and imposed on my own children too heavily. I had always known myself to be sunny, a truly happy person, and when Johnie stopped by and asked me seriously, "Are you happy?" I had to face my truth. I was no longer happy. I regretfully asked Dennis to move out. He was gracious and sweet, and told me I had taught him much about parenting. We said goodbye.

Through the years Johnie continued to call and continued to ask me to marry him, each time with promises of sobriety and stability—promises he was not capable of keeping. Finally he made plans to take me to find a house we could buy near the beach, and I was almost ready to believe we could do it, when he took off once more for the valley and his old drinking buddies. One night shortly after, he and a woman he befriended had a violent argument, and she ran over him with a truck, breaking most of the bones in his body. He barely survived, and he has struggled with the aftermath of pain ever since. The calls still come, but no longer does he call collect. In my journal I recorded Johnie's story:

Alco-cycle mood-swing
From gloom
to conversion
to playful, rowdy comedy,
to excessive, phony verbalization,
to maudlin self-pity,
to tears,
     SNAP!
to mindless rage,
to retching wretchedness,
to temporary oblivion,
to waking pain
     to gloom.

Watching a revival of the timeless musical "The Music Man" I listened to Miss Marion sing to the deceiving and manipulative Harold Hill:

There were birds all around
but I never heard them singing

I never heard them at all
till there was you.

And I was reminded that we sometimes gather flowers, even as we fight our way through life's brambles.

"I love you", he said, "I'm sorry".

Sorry? for loving? How can that be?

And through the painful years, I came to understand. Today, cutting away the brambles of an alcoholic's crazy-making drama, I cradle the flowers of a true and lasting love, and say, "Thank you for the music. I never heard it at all, till there was you".

Kristi was making movies—*Girls Just Want to Have Fun, Hard Bodies,* second lead in *Tomboy.* I was so proud, and so delighted to go to screenings with her. She met and fell in love with a handsome young Lebanese businessman named Jean el Kawas. After they had been in love for about a year, Jean was leaving work in the jewelry district of downtown Los Angeles on a Sunday afternoon, and was attacked and robbed in a parking lot, shot, and left for dead. He sustained wounds that left him paralyzed from the waist down. From his hospital bed, he urged Kristi to forget him and go on with her life, but she was not about to give up on her love. The two of them traveled to a spa behind the Iron Curtain, where they lived in one small room together hoping to find a cure for his paralysis. At the end of their stay, Jean went on to his homeland of Lebanon to visit his family, and Kristi came back to the US, grieving for him. I had feared my girl was infected with a "rescuer gene" and wanted to stay with this man "as long as he needs me", but now I saw that she truly loved him, so I supported her decision to marry him. They were married twice; once in Lebanon, and once in the UU church in Studio City with the Rev. Dori Somers officiating. They moved to San Fernando Valley.

In addition to the Riskins, Sharon and Gail, people I met through Carla Souter at "The Zone" included a magazine publisher and shop owner named Jeanette Zinkin, professionally named Mistress Antoinette. This businesswoman was also a dominatrix in "the scene", the world of dominance and submission or "S & M". Having been trained in teaching sex education, I investigated further and came to understand the psychology of this game. What made a strong, responsible person want to give up his power and play at being submissive in sexual games, or a submissive person to take control of the situation playing at dominance? I believe it was emotionally freeing and perhaps even restful. As clergy and a person of stature in the community, I was Jeanette's choice to sit on a TV panel she had been asked to assemble. I accepted her invitation and spoke on behalf of the folks who chose to express their sexuality in different ways—dressing in costumes, leather or rubber, cross-dressing, enjoying their particular fetishes, experimenting—always in mutually consenting adult relationships. I later helped out at Jeanette's shop and came to know transvestites and transsexuals, people who played with bondage or dressed in leather, those trying corsetry or medieval costumes, and I became their friend and their chaplain.

Jeanette introduced me to an artist who told her he thought I was "cute". His name was Gary Lee and he made miniatures for special effects in films; we began dating. Gary had a collection of rubber garments, and when we were going to a

143

party, he loaned me a black rubber dress with a mock turtle neckline and long bloused sleeves. It was very flattering and fun to wear. He bought me a stunning red and black rubber gown for Christmas. Unlike most non-clergy I'd dated, Gary was not intimidated by my profession and was actually proud to be with me, gladly chauffeuring me to speaking engagements, and accompanying me to weddings. Gary had been a conscientious objector during the Viet Nam war, and believed individuals and nations could live in harmony. We were highly compatible. He was, however, a bit overwhelmed by the never-alone, open house aspect of my life that filled my time and space with young people—my children and everyone else's! He liked helping the helpless and as a rescuer, he was easily swept into accepting a roommate in need who told me she was determined to land him as a husband. I eventually officiated at their wedding.

The publication of my book, *Weeds? Or Wildflowers!* was completed by Christmas of Amy's senior year. My dear friend Camille McCarthy held a book-signing party to honor the event, but the church members were lukewarm about their minister's gifts. Before Amy's graduation from high school, the Fullerton church hit a slump and failed to renew our covenant.

My first book!

I have always been pretty well organized, and it seemed to me I should be able to help others to organize themselves. I found another professional group that stimulated this idea for me. The writers of "how to" books and designers of closets—the organizers—were organized into their own organization. (This makes me smile!) And so my education continued. Dr. Michael Riskin was very good at psychotherapy, but not at all good at managing the business side of his professional life. His wife Anita gave him a present—me. She asked me to help Michael find things on his desk, file insurance claims promptly and pay his bills on time, in short, to get him organized. So I became Michael's business consultant and companion one day a week. He said my biggest gift to him was "being there", that I "inspirited" him. The loving connection, the being with, requires us to listen, to put ourselves in touch with the other person, to simply be, and to give the gift of total attention, to give our presence as a present. Perhaps I'd learned this from Linc, back in Stafford, so long ago.

Amy began her college studies at Cal State Fullerton, but hated the big school's impersonal atmosphere, so she transferred to Cypress College, and the two of us, with our dog Duchess, moved to an apartment on Brea Blvd. I began freelance writing and editing on a second-hand Apple computer. This was a step up from the old CPF hard drive and components I'd dubbed "Annie" because as an isolated old non-brand named computer, she was an antique orphan. One day, in the tradition of all our house room/heart room guests, Matt Budds materialized as a roommate in our little apartment. He was the young man championed by Amy's college classmate and adopted sibling, Danny, as "just right" for her; and apparently she agreed. He never questioned his welcome, nor did I. We loved him and welcomed him into our home and our hearts.

During a family discussion about the struggles for survival here in Fullerton, Mark asked me, "Where would you like to live, Mom?" and I began with, Kristi is in… and Amy…"No, Mom!" he said, "Where do *you* want to live?" "Oh", I said, "I've always wanted to live by the sea!" And so it was that Mark joined forces and resources with Amy, Matthew and me to rent and share a home in Huntington Beach.

Chapter sixteen
Sun, sand and surf

Harold Yoos, a classmate from high school, exchanged Christmas cards with me every year, and from his one life-long Mt. Holly address, he observed my peripatetic life in California, and called me a gypsy. My gypsy life however, has taught me to travel light. It has made me aware of how little it takes to make a home—my presence, my love and my aesthetic sense, heart room and hyacinths. Wherever I am fully present, there is home!

Looking at ads for rentals near the beach, we found that Huntington Beach offered the best possibilities, so we decided on beautiful Surf City, or "HB". A nearly new two-story house on a narrow lot about half a mile from the beach on California Street was listed for rent by the owners, who were moving to Florida. We loved the place, with its airy family room, gracious dining room and bedroom balcony, and we moved in. There were abundant bookshelves and a convenient study spot for me and my Mac overlooking the kitchen. A tiny patio and garden space separated the house from a two-car garage facing an alleyway. Our dog Duchess was so fastidious she used only a three-foot square of bare soil to potty. We were thrilled with the place. We were living at the beach!

The four of us had just gotten comfortably settled when, before six months passed, the owners took advantage of the month-to-month lease and gave us notice. Their Florida experiment had failed, and they needed their home back, so we had to find another place to live, immediately. Amy, Matt, Mark and I soon began to feel like professional house-hunters riding around HB and Fountain Valley, looking for a place we could afford. We finally spotted a four-bedroom house with a pool on Hightide, in the southeastern corner of the city, just blocks from the beach. No real estate personnel were around to show us the place, so Matt, the policeman's son, slipped in through a window and showed us the house. We tiptoed through, without disturbing a thing. This was definitely the place for us, so we contacted the landlord at once and made arrangements to move in. The front doors of the Hightide house opened into a large front room suitable for a shared office for Mark and me, with a huge family room and a dining room off a comfortable kitchen. My rattan basket swing was right at home beside the pool, hanging just outside my bedroom's French doors. A doggy door led in through my bathroom. Pretty cool for our dog, Duchess!

Once more, June decided to join the family in California. She looked for work as a nanny, sold Avon, and found her social circle at the Orange Coast UU Church, where she was happily welcomed into the choir. Birdie and Charlie introduced her to a young man named Ken Cook who was active on their social justice committee. June and Ken were just right for each other and got better acquainted in a play-reading group from the church. True soulmates, they fell in love and Ken joined the Hightide family.

Mark had been working in a dead-end job for my friend Carla's parents. One of his good buddies invited him to spend a week at deBenneville Pines as an adult counselor at Senior High Camp, and he found his new calling. He gathered teens around him before the fireplace, read aloud from *Winnie the Pooh*, and generally became a Pied Piper to the kids. He was a born teacher, even as he had always been a born writer. In addition to discovering himself at deBenneville, Mark discovered another counselor, Christy Cathcart, whom he thought might be the girl for him. She was dating someone else at the time, so that connection had to wait a little while, but while we were living in HB, she spent some time with us, and found that this man and his family just might be right for her. Mark began supplementing his college degree, working toward a teaching certificate while substitute teaching in Garden Grove.

I worked at editing and manuscript doctoring in our front room office, and went out on consulting and organizing assignments at Riskin Banker and for my friend Camille McCarthy, who'd inherited quite a bit of real estate to manage, when her husband died. I also produced the company newsletter and conducted team-building exercises with LACERA, the Los Angeles County Employees Retirement Association in downtown LA, and after their move, in Pasadena. I took on the position of Regional Director for "The Network" a collection of community based networking clubs in Orange and LA counties, which required my attendance at 7:00 AM meetings from Newport to Redondo Beach.

Dr. George Fields, who had been a member of the Fullerton church while he was in med school,, introduced me to an elderly Egyptian physician from Long Beach, who wanted his poetry edited and prepared for publication, The work was tedious, but the old doctor was delightful. He always left me with the blessing, "May God bless you rrrrichly"

Another Long Beach resident who needed my editorial help was a husband and father who'd written a book he titled *The Umbrella Man*, about his inside knowledge of a Kennedy assassination conspiracy involving a real person, a policeman from Long Beach. He would bring me one chapter and then the next, and I'd rewrite each to make it readable. His wife's delighted response to my work was, "Now that reads like a real book!" He was launching a business that involved computerizing and consolidating medical records to make them retrievable anywhere, something that has become ordinary for medical groups in today's electronic age. He wanted me to join his sales staff, which was not the sort of thing I could picture myself doing. He paid me well for my editorial work, but before he could sell his manuscript, he suddenly disappeared, along with his proposed business venture and his dangerous exposé.

Kristi and Jean bought a house on a hillside in Encino, with a motorized wrought iron gate and a pathway from the house up to a hilltop rock garden. Jean had not been accustomed to having a dog, but he was about to experience a new kind of love. Kristi got a black Labrador puppy whose lineage demanded a name associated with firearms, and they named him Magnum. He was the sweetest of animals. When Jean and Kristi made a trip to Lebanon, they sent Magnum to stay with us in HB, and I became his second mother. He was not a jumper, but whenever he saw me he would gently put his paws on my shoulders to give me a doggy hug.

The Academy Awards have been a high-holy-day event for our family for years. When *Silence of the Lambs* and Anthony Hopkins won, Mark and Amy wouldn't take "no" for an answer when they brought home the video for my viewing. I didn't want to watch this scary movie, but as an obedient parent, I did. OK, it was a good film. Later, when we found ourselves scattered and unable to watch together as the stars paraded on the red carpet, a telephone brigade naturally formed. When a really ghastly outfit showed up on the screen, my phone would ring during the next commercial break, and I'd hear Kristi or Amy asking, "What was she thinking? Doesn't she have a sister?" Clearly, in our world a sister would always intervene to prevent her sibling from making such bad fashion decisions. Familial loyalty protects!

In the summer of '91, Bill Foster from the Unitarian Universalist church in Whittier called and asked me to meet with their search committee. During the interviews, I was surprised at the ease with which I was able to answer difficult questions about churchmanship, social justice, congregational harmony and growth. Twenty years of ministering had taught me more than I realized. I had become a mensch, and perhaps an elder. Someday I might even become the "holy woman" Dr. George Fields anointed me. Or not. They called me to their pulpit in September 1991.

The stories all ministers tell most often are those about the weddings at which they have officiated. I call the recounting of mine "Oh, the many men I've married". I've been guilty from time to time of misleading references to "one of the men

I've married." And sometimes—stranger still—to one of the women. I may have gotten the impulse to such corny wit from my brother-in-law, the pediatrician, who sometimes pointed out local women as the mothers of his children. Doc also had an ambiguous compliment he used for the less than beautiful child. He would simply say, "Now, there's a baby!"

In over thirty years of ministry, a lot of weddings have become grist for this storyteller's mill. Some remind me sweetly of why I became a minister, and others have given me pause or even cause to doubt the call. Once, prior to a wedding scheduled for that acoustical wonder of a chapel, "the onion", I met with the groom, the bride and her gentle father, who had raised her alone. Plans were completed in a pleasant atmosphere of cooperation. During the week prior to the wedding, however, I received a phone call, a strange woman's voice, demanding certain changes in the wedding plan. "Who are you?" I asked, and was informed this was the bride's long estranged mother. "I make changes only at the request of the bride", I told her. At the wedding rehearsal, I discovered the woman had taken over the decoration of the church, filling the tiny room with enough flowers, archways and other accouterments to grace a cathedral. As I was guiding the wedding party through their tableau, the erstwhile mother loudly attempted to direct the procedure. I quietly removed her from the sanctuary. Sadly, no one was available to remove the woman from the bride's wedding day experience. The girl became so overwrought by the re-entry of her difficult parent into her life, she dealt with the stress by popping a few pills. I learned of this sad state of affairs as the bride came swaying unsteadily down the aisle, giggling and waving at her stunned family and friends.

Another disaster had as its venue the Disneyland Hotel gazebo, where the about-to-be mother-in-law, a highly verbal New Yorker, played havoc with the rehearsal, the bride's nerves and the celebration. As we sat in a selected restaurant, she suddenly reneged on her commitment to pay for the rehearsal dinner. I quietly left the restaurant and headed home unfed, thinking, "Oh, that poor bride". And then came the wedding day. I arrived at the site half an hour early, and discovered the bride swearing like a stevedore and holding up the ceremony for two hours, out of sheer cussedness. That young groom, it seems, had jumped out of the proverbial frying pan. Ah, well.

Not long after that "Why am I putting myself through all this?" experience, I received another phone call. This one royally redeemed my ministerial calling. Gloria, the bride, was in her sixties, and had spent most of her long married years smoothing life's rough spots caused by an alcoholic husband. When her spouse died, friends insisted on introducing Gloria to "J. B.", a nice gentleman who had spent the final seven years of his marriage caring for a seriously ill invalid wife. In a lovely twist of fate, it happened that Gloria and J. B. had grown up in neighboring towns in Texas fifty years before. As a girl she'd had a long-distance crush on him, the rival school's football star. It was love at first and second sight for the couple, and for their families as well. Here were two good people who deserved romance and happiness, and we were all blessed to be a part of that. This is what ministry is supposed to be about!

There have been times throughout the years when I have married the same couple more than once. One lovely middle-aged pair, the Kays, had been married some years before, and then divorced. Early in the marriage, he had strayed and she had promptly arranged for them to become "unmarried". Shortly after the divorce, however, Mrs. Kay contracted polio and needed care—which Mr. Kay moved in at once to provide. They had been together ever since. When the couple met with me she wanted to be remarried, but he suggested that was a bad idea because they had failed at marriage. "No", I said, "It's divorce you were not good at. You two have done what a strong, loving married couple does; you have weathered the storm, given mutual forgiveness and support, then gone on to grow together". On the 19th anniversary of their first wedding, I remarried them. And five years later they asked me to celebrate with them once more, renewing the vows that held true meaning for them both.

Other multiple weddings have grown out of the wish of a couple to do the "big wedding thing" sometime later for the benefit of family and friends, along with the need or desire to get married here and now for one reason or another. It is of no importance if the state papers have been filed long since, so long as the marriage is beautifully spoken and joyously celebrated. Happily, that's my job!

The most recent of my harrowing tales stars the Reverend as comic relief. Following my own advice to nascent brides, I have recognized that my embarrassing episode would make a good story, and "If it's going to be funny in a year; let it be funny now!" The bride wanted to be wed on the way from Newport Beach to Catalina Island, "rocked in the cradle of the deep", so to speak. We boarded her friend's 48-foot cruiser at 9:00 in the morning, and set off into the June gloom of a misty sea. As a canvas sailor accustomed to the ocean waves and a girl of Norwegian descent, I'd never considered seeking a seasick preventative, and I repeatedly denied the squeamish symptoms my body broadcast as I gazed into the horizonless distance. Then I made the mistake of drinking an offered cup of orange juice, and my tummy rebelled! I was in awe at the efficiency of the muscular rejection of that beverage and of the coffee and muffin that had preceded it. I continued to smile and to assure the boat's owner that I was just fine. She brought me a 7-up, and that soon followed the orange juice over the rail. Then the motor slowed and stopped. We were at the spot chosen for the ceremony. I sat on the top of the forward cabin to keep from being tossed overboard by the rolling of the boat, and spoke the lovely words of the couple's wedding covenant, light-headed but clear-voiced and calm. They had written their own ring vows, and as I handed off the ceremonial book to the groom, my unruly interior catapulted me to the rail once more. Then back I "crawled" to the couple, to finish the wedding and bless them. "What a trouper!" they said. And what a story this will make! And so it is!

June and Ken decided to leave California and head for the east coast, stopping off to visit Ken's friends in Virginia, then on to Maine, where his parents and brother lived. They found an apartment in the old library building in Bangor, as neighbors to my beloved friend Dr. Jerry Metz, and Junie once again became a letter writer.

On my sixtieth birthday Amy, Mark and Matt came up with a lovely idea for a gift. They found a beautiful bentwood rocker like one I'd had years before, from Grandma White, Buz's grandmother. I'd nursed my babies in that old chair, and this one would look really nice in our family room. What the dears didn't count on was the scary quality of a sixtieth birthday. I freaked! Somehow, a rocking chair represented to me everything I was not—sedentary, stuffy, out to pasture, and old. They graciously removed the offending object, and gave me something else far more acceptable and far less memorable. I don't remember what it was.

In a charming old-fashioned but modern way, Matt and Amy piled onto my bed with me one night and he asked for my daughter's hand in marriage. Of course I said yes. The wedding was to be in a year, and my efficient Miss Amy arranged for the reception to be held in the community hall in Costa Mesa, which was so much in demand, only a Sunday was left open. "It's OK", she said, "We can be married on a Sunday; I have an in with the minister". "Uncle Charlie" and "Aunt Birdie" claimed membership rights at Orange Coast Church, so we had use of the sanctuary for the ceremony as family of members. Because her beloved brother had been the man of her family for most of her life, Amy asked Mark to escort her, and because he was her father whom she loved, she asked Irving also. Together, the two men walked with her down the aisle.

Amy and Matt brought home a puppy. Having a large dog already, I'd have been reluctant to welcome another pet, and had I been given veto power, I'd have used it. Luckily she just appeared, a little white ball of fluff. Matt took her to work with him and his coworkers asked, "What's that?" "She's a Lhasa Apso", he told them. "Oh, a Lasa Vegas". they said. And so she was named Lucky Lady Las Vegas, to be called Vegas. Wherever Duchess ran, Vegas chased behind; that was her job. She adopted a shelf built into my computer cart, on which to sleep while I worked, and although she was Amy and Matt's pup, she bonded with Duchess and with me. As the time for the wedding and the couple's exodus approached,

I began to worry about the little dog. They would be living in a small apartment and working all day, leaving her alone. The poor little thing would be without either Duchess or me, and really lonely. About a week before the wedding, Amy asked me if I would be willing to keep Vegas, and I breathed a huge sigh of relief. But on the day before Amy and Matt's wedding, Vegas disappeared. The uproar in the house was epic until she was finally found at the county shelter and brought home. Thankfully the wedding wasn't shattered by the tragedy of a lost friend. The tiny dancer was my roommate and treasured companion for the rest of her sixteen-year life.

Mark, June, Amy, Dori and Kristi

Amy invited her wedding attendants to spend the night before the wedding in our home, which we considered a perfect house from which to marry. Instead of raucous partying, Matt and his best friend, Donny George visited awhile with the girls, then went out into the neighborhood and "raided" the overhanging rosebushes all along the sidewalk, gathering rose petals for the flower girl's basket. Such bandits! Amy wore her mother's wedding dress adding her special beauty to the 1953 treasure. Aunt June and Uncle Doc brought Amy's beloved Meme across country by air, and they graced her wedding, as they had graced Kristi's. Because both the bride and the groom were persons of stature, this little minister brought a step-master to the church and draped it in white sheeting, to stand upon and look into the couple's eyes.

I grew up in a home full of smooches, hugs, and cuddles—from mother, father, sister, aunt and uncle—a home where laughter and warmth were part of the "health food" for our growing. This is also the way I created a home for my family. Years later, as Director of the senior high summer camp in the beautiful Berkshires, I became part of another family that recognized the beauty of an embrace—the children! And here in southern California I often wore my camp T-shirt emblazoned with the title, "Hug Therapist", because campers at deBenneville Pines also treasure the gift of hugs, with meaning! That little blue scoop-necked shirt brought me a bounty of delight one day in the local dentist's office. As I stood waiting for my next appointment to be scheduled, a tiny ancient face peered up into mine, and a lady of many years requested the therapy of my hug. I was honored to give it warmly and with joy.

One day a letter arrived from Valerie White. It began, "I'm sure I'm the last person you'd ever hope to hear from, but..." She told me this was a letter honoring me for the way I live my life, and thanking me for my honesty and grace in a difficult situation. She had just decided to make use of the "freedom of information" act, and had requested the records of her application for a job as a US border guard. The report dated back to when we lived in Van Nuys. One evening while living on Enadia Way, I was preparing dinner when my doorbell rang. Knife in hand, I went to the door. How strange! There was an FBI agent requesting information about someone named Valerie White, married to Irving Stevens. I truly believed no one would ever know what I said to this man. Who could anticipate such a thing as that? Everything I said, I believed to be between me and the agent who questioned me. But the very person I'd been questioned about was now free to read the government report of the interview.

"I'm sorry", I told him, that night. "I can't give you an unbiased evaluation of Ms. White. I can verify that my husband left me to move in with her but I have nothing else to tell you". Did she drink to excess he asked. "No" or have money problems? "No". Would she be a threat to the United States? "Certainly not!" And as to her personal character? "I am not qualified to make that judgment, but you mustn't assume that means something bad. I was her minister, and anything she told me in that capacity I cannot and will not talk about, but I do recommend her for the position of border guard, and I believe she will serve the country faithfully". From the woman I was expected to despise I had just learned that I've been living according to what I teach. This is how I define belief. Belief manifests in what you do, how you live. Anything less is just talk. Emerson said, "Your actions speak so loudly, I cannot hear what you say." And I remember Mark's insight in Stafford about parents teaching by the way they choose to live. Thank God I learned that and made it part of my life!

Amy's summer vacations had been trips back east to visit with her father, and she traveled as an unescorted minor, accompanied by a cluster of small surprise gifts to open one by one, helping to pass the time, along with a small companion— lovable, furry old Grover of the Muppets. A simple little plaque, the souvenir gift bought with hoarded pennies by my small daughter during her summer away, graced my office or bedroom for many years. She chose it because "it reminded me of you, Mom". The words are from Emerson:

> Do not follow where the path may lead.
> Go, instead, where there is no path, and leave a trail.

How powerful are the messages of the life we live, even when we may not be aware.

Shortly after Amy and Matt left, Mark and Christy found an apartment in Redondo Beach, and set up housekeeping where they could see the ocean from their balcony. The big house on Hightide was empty and expensive, and finding rentals with two dogs was not easy. Unable to find a tenant to share the cost of the house, I moved to a townhouse on the west side of town.

Chapter seventeen
On my own

For as long as I'd had my own living space, mine had been a house full of young people, and now I was living alone for the first time in my life. I had yet to learn how to enjoy solitude and appreciate my own company, so my attractive townhouse apartment seemed lonely and depressing. Duchess and Vegas took me on walks, and I commuted to the Whittier church easily enough, but soon I felt something close to panic at the emptiness, and began looking for a place in the valley, close to Kristi and Jean. At about the time I located a rental in Encino, they moved to Northridge, across the valley, but the house seemed right for me, and I moved once more. Needing some help with the costs of the rental, and having a second bedroom to spare, I advertised in the Studio City church newsletter for a roommate. A mature gentleman named David Frost applied, and I checked with my friends at the church as to the advisability of taking him in as a tenant. The response was very positive, and David moved in. He soon became like an adopted brother. Because it makes me happy to feed people, we shared meals as well as household space.

A room off the kitchen had a view of the back garden with its fruit trees and picnic table. I made this room my office and began work on a special project for the Whittier congregation, a cookbook. We titled it *Wow! That Tastes Good; How Do You Make It?* and I had a wonderful time designing the layout, adding witty sayings and finding great graphics. It was a wonderful vehicle for preserving Isaksen family recipes along with those of the church folk. In addition to my ministry at Whittier, I did some advertising art for Jean's businesses and joined the Chamber of Commerce in pursuit of communications clients.

Whittier UU Church had been meeting in the Whitmore YWCA for some years and the commute from Encino was longer than it had been from Huntington Beach. One Sunday morning I made some final notes and adjustments to the morning's sermon, carefully put out my worship materials and prepared to leave for church. When I began to pack my briefcase I couldn't find my sermon manuscript so I ran off a replacement copy and headed for Whittier. Somehow I'd gotten my internal calendar confused and thought this was the "first Sunday", when we would meet early for a breakfast, but I was wrong. Arriving an hour too early, I picked up the Sunday paper near the locked door to the "Y", sat on the bench in front of the building, and read the funnies and the local news. When I went inside to set up for church, I discovered I had everything with me but a sermon. I was frantic. I searched through my materials page by page, but there was no manuscript to be found. I'd been delivering sermons from a manuscript for twenty years, but I walked into the pulpit that morning with nothing, not even notes, and began to wing it. Amazingly, the congregation loved it! After church someone went out front and looked at the bench where I'd been reading the news, and there was my sermon, complete and unruffled. Was the cosmos telling me something? The proper ending to the story would be that I got the message and began preaching without a script, but I wasn't that quick. It took me another year or more before I learned about mind maps, and ventured forth into the uncharted scriptless wilderness. But I did learn, eventually.

Amy and Matt were about to start their family, and sweetly made their announcement to me as a special Easter surprise. I was so self-involved at the moment however that I only saw that I was the last person on their list to learn of the coming blessed event. Unrelated friends already knew, and I let myself react from my hurt feelings instead of the joy I really felt for them. Of such mistakes are family heartbreaks often made, but I admitted my failing and we rejoiced together from then on.

Mark and Christy planned their wedding in Pasadena in the garden of UU Neighborhood Church with Mark's Mom officiating along with Christy's friend Laurie, the Pasadena assistant minister. Matt and a sweetly rounded Amy sang during the ceremony and Kristi sang at the reception. Aunt June and Uncle Doc were determined to be at the wedding and came across the continent against doctors' orders. Bud was fighting pancreatic cancer, and June was fighting breast cancer. They joked about "his and hers oncologists", and about overdoing togetherness. Meme was in an assisted living facility near Burlington County Memorial and not able to travel. Uncle Doc continued to call our freeways "Fwees" because of the FWY abbreviation, and June laughed heartily at the many banks in San Fernando Valley, especially when a tree-shaded sign seemed to read Preschool Bank. It turned out to be a partially hidden sign for the Montessori Preschool of Burbank.

Christy and Mark had their honeymoon in Hawaii, and not long after their return announced that they, too, would be parents, about six months after the Budds. Kristi had been undergoing exhausting fertility procedures for five years, attempting in vitro fertilization, and one morning she called to tell me the great news that the procedure had been successful at last. She was pregnant! Joy reigned; this was to be a year of wonderful babies. As was our custom, we had our family Thanksgiving together at the Kawas house, expecting Amy to go into labor at any time. That Sunday the first "grand" was born in Long Beach Memorial Hospital. Praise is for the changes in maternity practices! Her husband and the two grandmothers, with sister Kristi, brother Mark and his Christy, supported Amy through her labor and friends Shelley and Shannon close by. Justin Daniel Budds, born on November 28, 1993, brought in the new generation of love.

One January morning very early I thought Duchess must be scratching herself while leaning against my bed; but the shaking didn't stop, and there was crashing and banging and an eerie roar as dishes leapt from the closets and mirrors crashed to the floor. Vegas's little heart beat so hard it seemed about to explode. This was the Northridge Quake. Aftershocks came regularly and made a lot of noise. David and I joined the neighbors in the street. My fears were all about the safety of Jean in his chair, and Kristi with her longed for pregnancy. When word came through that they were safe across the valley, I relaxed and started to clean up the mess.

About six months later, it was becoming a struggle once more for me to make ends meet, and the Budds were hoping to move into a house of their own. They came to my aid with an offer of shared living, so that instead of paying rent to a stranger, I was privileged to help a little with the housing costs, pay a gardener and cleaning service and spend nearly two years bonding with my first grandchild. I moved to Whittier with Amy, Matt, and Justin plus the two dogs.

Christy Lynn and Mark were living in Fountain Valley and scheduled to have their baby in May at Hoag Memorial Hospital, Newport Beach. On the twentieth, the day I was to officiate at a wedding in Burbank, Christy went into labor, as the time came for me to head north on the freeway. I reached the mountainside venue for the ceremony, scrambled down a gully and up a steep incline, married the couple, scrambled back down the incline and up the gully, and into my car. I raced back to Newport, and arrived just as baby Caitlin was brought out from her first bath, ready to meet the world.

Our third treasure arrived mid-July in the somewhat earthquake-damaged Northridge Hospital, welcomed by what seemed to be the entire Lebanese community of Los Angeles plus his grandmothers, aunts and uncles. The cultural differences between these gregarious and communal Mediterranean folk and our individualistic and private Americans made for occasional misunderstandings, but the beautiful dark-eyed baby boy was a miracle of love for all of us. Elias Salim Kawas was the third member of our mini-mod squad.

My nephews always call me Dee. When Larry was learning to speak, his first word was not Mommy nor DaDa, but

Dee. It was supposed to be Auntie Dee, at first, but the boys thought of me as their teen-aged aunt, even at 25, 30, or 50 so the "auntie" part went by the wayside. With the arrival of grandchildren I thought I would probably be called Grandma Dee, but as Justin began talking, he simply called me DeeDee, and so it was. When Justin was two years old it was time for me to move on, and I had managed to save a bit of money toward that move. I looked at mobile home parks in the valley, and wondered about the size of a coach I had seen advertised. On the way to visit my friend Sharon, I passed a mobile home salesroom, and stopped in to see for myself what the smallest units felt like from the inside. A salesman offered to show me a new double wide, and I said, "No thank you, I couldn't afford one".

"What if I could show you how to afford one?" he asked. Then he told me a space had just become available in Huntington Shorecliffs, a park I had admired and longed to inhabit when living in HB. They were about to tow away a disreputable old thing overrun with beer cans, and they could put a brand new cottage in its place, just for me. When I talked with Jean about this opportunity, he offered me $10,000 toward the down payment to make it possible. When I asked how and when I could repay such an amount, he said it was a gift, not a loan. I am forever grateful.

My new home was Wedgwood blue with white trim, and it sat just across from the park office and swimming pool—number 113, the same number as my family's phone number at Road's End. The question of how long I might be able to afford this place was diminished for me by the joy I felt in having my own house at the beach, for even a little while. Because Justin was accustomed to DeeDee always being there, we carefully prepared him for my move, telling him about the house, taking him on a tour of it before the move, then bringing him to see me settled as soon as the moving van drove away. I assured him this was to be his house, too, and he could stay here with me anytime he wanted to visit. I was once more living at the beach.

Chapter eighteen
Back to the beach

What makes life meaningful? Beautiful? Joyful? Fun? Why are we sometimes so slow to recognize the delight to be found in our own works and simple pleasures? Why not rejoice in even a brief delight!

The neighbors in Huntington Shorecliffs were overjoyed to have a brand new, beautiful cottage where once had been an ugly derelict. My next-door neighbor was the mystery author, Audrey Peterson, and we became friends at once. She alternated between living in California and in Bellingham Washington. Her daughters, one of whom suffered from bipolar disorder, visited regularly when she was in town.

I planted a garden in front of the house, and put white garden furniture on the porch. I found a glider swing for the tiny back patio, and stored my tools in the blue and white mini-barn. I planted herbs in huge pots, and a Meyer lemon tree in the side yard. The place was my pride and joy. When preparing for the move to Shorecliffs, I had found a small armchair and ottoman upholstered in rose-colored velveteen. It became my reading and TV-viewing chair, comfortable for a "grand" in my lap and Vegas snuggled at my feet with her chin on my ankles.

I began taking Vegas regularly to Edison Park for her morning walk, and there we met lots of wonderful dog people. I became friends with Kay and Dan Ozsvath, and their adorable Westies, MacDuff, Molly and Max. Vegas was friendly with the other dogs in the park, but snobbishly ignored their humans. When she was at home, however, she was the ultimate hostess, offering a welcome dance whenever I told her, "We've got company!" She became part of the pre-wedding interviews I did with couples I was going to marry, running out to greet them when they arrived, and dancing them into the house. When Justin spent the night at DeeDee's house, we would visit the playground portion of Edison Park next morning, "sailing" in the pirate ship, with Justin playing Captain Hook, and DeeDee as Mr. Smee. We played on the swings and slides, and rescued tennis balls from outside the courts, listened to the gulls and wondered why they didn't "laugh" as their cousins on the Atlantic shore had done.

A second round of babies blessed our family— David William Carter Somers was born on July 2, 1996; named for Mark's cousin and a college friend, for William Shakespeare, and for Mark's father, O. Carter Somers, Jr. Mark and family were by then living north of San Francisco in Rohnert Park and they were greatly missed in Southern California. Next came the Kawas twins, Laura Marie and Michael Charles, born January 10, 1997, followed by Madeline Jeanine Budds born on March 11, 1997, and carrying forth the happy theme of "Lilac time".

Mark's friend and mentor from his teaching days in Orange County was Marlys Nelson, who lived in Seacliff, an elegant apartment complex across Beach Blvd. from the mobile home park where I lived. She invited me to join the Friends of the Huntington Beach Library, and suggested to the executive board that they hire me to produce their monthly newsletter, an assignment I enjoyed immensely. The most fun was checking out the delightful array of imaginative jewelry, decorative items and toys in the Library Gift Shop, then writing the ad copy. We sponsored monthly luncheons with Orange County authors as guest speakers, including such outstanding writers as T. Jefferson Parker, Earlene Fowler, and Elizabeth George.

When 1997 began,, my ministry to the Whittier Congregation ended and I officially retired and became a lifetime member of continental UUMA. A phone call from an unknown person in the offices of Royal Caribbean Cruise Line surprised me with an offer to officiate at on-board weddings. I never discovered who had recommended me, but this was a fine opportunity, and a beautiful manifestation of *Divine Abundance*. In the program called Royal Romance a couple would book a honeymoon cruise, then purchase the wedding package which included flowers, champagne, pictures and cake. I would perform a legal California marriage before the ship left port, then leave the ship and return to my four-legged roommate, Vegas, for a snuggle. I agreed to this arrangement, and at the behest of the cruise line officials, invested in becoming a Notary Public, so that I could also issue licenses, if needed. This turned out to be unnecessary, a waste of time and money, as Notaries in California do not have the same rules and duties as those in Florida, where the company is headquartered. The clientele for the shipboard weddings was very different from the couples I'd been accustomed to marrying, but some of them were sweet and likable, and the sailing staff were always delightful. As with ministry anywhere, there were stories generated by drunken brides, wicked mothers-in-law, and careless companions, but one event almost inspired me to write a mystery novel. The bride and groom for one of my weddings failed to appear at the scheduled time and couldn't be found anywhere on the vessel. Although they had checked through boarding clearance they never showed up at their cabin, nor did they respond to pages. I thought this was a great beginning for a mystery story, but I had to disembark at 4:00 PM so I missed the rest of the story. Evidently the couple had not met with disaster, but were hiding, trying to avoid paying for a wedding they had decided to postpone or cancel.

A friend invited me to attend services at the Church of Religious Science in Huntington Beach on a Sunday when I was not in a Unitarian Universalist pulpit. I was moved by the message, thrilled by the music and inspired by the preaching. The Rev. Mary Murray Shelton was dynamic and beautiful in her presentation, and became a model for me of what a preacher could be. Later in our association, she told me how to use a mind map and forgo the old manuscript for delivering a sermon. The lesson begun in Whittier almost two years before came full circle. I also took a course of spiritual study with Mary, and found support for my beliefs about the sacred oneness of the cosmos, and our universal connectedness. When Mary succumbed to a serious back injury, she moved north to Sebastopol and Peggy Price, her associate, was called to become senior minister. She had just completed her training as CRS clergy, and did an amazing job in a very challenging situation. A friend said, "Peggy didn't know the task she had undertaken couldn't be done, so she just did it". Don't we all sometimes find ourselves called to do the same? I came to think of Peggy as a little sister, treasuring her gentle spirit, which pervaded the church in HB.

I have sometimes described myself as a Relational Humanist—it is my own term or label—and it means to me that I find wholeness in a trio or "Unitarian trinity" of relationships. I must be in relationship with the self, at peace, centered; I must be in relationship with God, the cosmos, the life force, the sacred; and I must be in relationship with the people in my life, my brothers and sisters. If any of the three is neglected I am broken and damaged, and have work to do, and like all of us, I always have work to do!

Melissa Blackburn, a young friend from San Fernando Valley said she wished I would teach a Women's Spirituality Class, and Kristi thought it a great idea. She encouraged me, so I began mind-mapping the concepts I might like to teach. I surprised myself with the richness of the drawings that sprang from my hand. Had I been living in the valley, I'd have offered this class in the Women's Center or The Learning Tree, but I was in HB. My doctor and dear friend, George Fields, had just opened his own office in Los Alamitos and wanted to offer a holistic array of services, so he encouraged me to present my Woman Spirit Seminar in his office suite. I outlined and offered classes one evening a week for 10 weeks. Dr. Fields sponsored his nurses and receptionist among the first students, and a bouquet of others came—a physician, a Hispanic prison guard, a purchasing agent, an optometrist, a retired office worker. The mix was refreshing and stimulating, and I was thrilled to watch "my girls" blossom. When the ten weeks were done, the women wanted more, so we continued to meet for some months longer. My friend Gail had joined the class, and we became ever closer. She had grown to be a lovely woman, and I found her to be among the most generous people I'd ever known. She lived a fair distance away, and I treasured the times we were able to be together.

The cosmos does provide. Whenever I'm working on a particular theme or topic I find that new insights about that subject flow in to enrich my life. I marveled at the wealth of material that appeared as I created exercises for the Woman Spirit class—stories, pictures, challenges and poems to share. I walked with Vegas through Edison Park and the sudden reappearance of the mountains in the distance after months of smog took my breath away. My muse said to me, *Epiphanies of Mountains*, and a poem was born. I drove along Beach Boulevard and noticed a tavern with a sign naming it a Certified Sports Bar, and I wondered what one would do to get a bar certified. Next time I passed the place, I looked more closely and realized my mind had jumped to mistaken conclusions, as the place was actually named Centerfield Sports Bar. What a fun learning story that was. I began to think, "if it's not fun, I may not be doing it right". Teaching this class was surely fun, and one of the most meaningful things I had done in my long ministry, with the learning, as always, a two-way street.

As a child I got the message loud and clear that I was no singer. When my children came along, however, I discovered the joyous acceptance little ones give their parent's melodies. I boldly sang old favorites and lullabies to them as we rocked in Grandma White's old bentwood rocker. Later, I sang with them, bouncing along in our red Ford Bronco. After a glass of wine, I even sang with colleagues around the piano—old Sunday school hymns fondly remembered.

And that Sunday back in Maine I actually sang alone in church. Amazingly, the notes were true, my voice was sweet, and the congregation loved it. But I still heard echoes of taunting laughter from the grown-ups in my head. Today, with my hair turned silver and my pipes a little rusty, I sing only in my car—alone! It crossed my mind as I was preparing a presentation some time ago, "It's too bad I can't sing". And then my muse stepped in with a message for me:

They Said I Couldn't Sing

They said I couldn't sing.
I know they loved me
yet they said I couldn't sing.
I had no song.
Their laughter chastened me;
my voice amused them
when I struggled for the tune
or notes went wrong.
My sister's tones were sweet,
her music welcomed.
She, thinking I couldn't sing,
shared poetry.
I went from memorizing
words to writing,
not yet understanding
words would set me free.
From time to time
a nonsense song or ditty,
a lullaby or hymn would

set me singing.
But always poems
germinated, blossomed
beneath my pen,
their strong life lessons bringing.
When Truth embraced me
I learned I am Spirit
expressing beauty.
Old messages were wrong.
I need not yearn for
melodies to warble.
My very life is music;
I am the song.

Birdie and Charlie Reed had moved from Fullerton to a beautiful house in Huntington Beach two blocks from the ocean on Fifteenth Street. They began traveling around the country enjoying their retirement, and were away fairly often. Birdie's mother, Ethel Smith, was living in Vintage Newport, an assisted living facility near Hoag Hospital, and when the Reeds were on the road I had the privilege of being Ethel's surrogate daughter, and visiting regularly with her, sharing my writings with her, and lunching with her in the gracious dining room of the Vintage. Ethel had a cat named Calamity Jane or CJ, and Birdie had arranged for full-time caregivers to keep her comfortable, but it was important to both of them that she have contact with a family presence daily. It gave me great joy to be with this wise and gracious lady, and to hear her stories. She lived to be 95 and I was privileged to celebrate her life at a memorial service.

My friend Sharon had suffered with diabetes since she was a girl, and her life was largely scheduled around her doctors' appointments. Her significant other or life partner for many years was Bruce Lackey, who was employed by Hewlett Packard, and so not available for taxi duty. Sharon was considered legally blind and could not drive herself to hospitals and doctors' offices, so I frequently accompanied her. She was beloved by all the medical personnel, and was known for her quirky sense of humor and willingness to share a joke. Sharon always remembered to send a birthday card, and often wrote little notes even to the mothers of her friends. When Bruce retired, he took over the driving duties and has cared for her through years of ill health and trauma.

While I was a young working woman, living with my parents in Cherry Hill, Papa found a pattern for a three and a half foot tall decorative Santa Claus, and cut it from a piece of plywood. I painted the old saint's face and his red suit, and Papa perched him on the chimney of "The Birches" for the holiday season. When I had my own home Saint Nick came to live with me, and he has ushered in my holidays and those of my children ever since. My kids grew up with Santa decorating our roof or our front door every Christmas throughout their lives. So in 1998 I decided to surprise my children and grandchildren with a hand-made Christmas present for each family. I copied and lengthened the pattern for Santa Claus and my dear Gail found a handyman who cut out three plywood forms for me. Then she helped with the basic painting and I created the familiar faces, so that they all looked just like the Santa we had always known and loved. I surprised the three California families, each with their own Mr. Claus. For June and Ken in their tiny apartment, supportive dollars were the more appropriate and preferred gift.

Santa and the "Grands"

While we were living in Fullerton, the Wyckoffs moved to
Corrales New Mexico, where they built an adobe version of
a Mediterranean villa. They worked to establish a Unitarian
Universalist church in nearby Rio Rancho, and Marj became
active in the historical society while John taught the local
police how to computerize their communication system.
From time to time John would use his frequent flyer credits
to fly me to Albuquerque, and pick me up at the airport for
a visit at their beautiful home. When their daughter-in-law
was killed in an auto accident and some years later, when
their son died by his own hand, they brought me to Corrales
to conduct the memorial services. My flights to New Mexico
were treasured times for me, and important sustenance to my
dear friends, the Wyckoffs.

Flying to visit Mark and Christy Lynn in Santa Rosa was less practical than driving, because I could easily take along gifts or books in the car and still make the trip in eight hours. By air, the one hour flight time portion on the plane was the least of the trip. Travel to the airport, from the parking lot, and by shuttle from Oakland to Santa Rosa, then by Mark's car from the shuttle station added another four or five hours, so the saving in time was minimal. I drove. I entertained myself with books on tape, and since Christy always made Vegas welcome, had the company of my little four-legged friend. Those visits were always memorable for the time I had with the "grands" I didn't see often enough, and for the "dates" with Mark (usually to the theatre) and with Christy (usually visiting some glorious garden or doing girl stuff).

After Uncle Doc's death, Aunt June, with her cancer in remission, found support in grief counseling groups, and became the lady to know for grieving gentlemen in the group. She found love and support with Charles, a handsome gent from Burlington and enjoyed a quick trip to Paris with him as well as time at the beach in the shadow of Old Barney. On two occasions she came to California and visited with me in my lovely beach home getting to play with the Southern California grandbabies, then riding with me to Santa Rosa to visit the northern kiddies. She moved from the house in Mt. Holly where she and Doc had lived for forty years, and bought a charming mobile home on a lake, which was visited by northern geese and a great blue heron. When Meme died at age 95, we gathered in June's living room with immediate family plus numerous cousins refusing to be limited by labels like first, second, or "once removed", and we were grateful to be family. After several years June's cancer returned. She wore a lavender wig to chemo and made her fellow sufferers laugh. Her hair left, and then began to return with an added curl. She sometimes wore a natural looking silvery wig, and sometimes chose to go *au naturel*, but she was always lovely.

Chapter nineteen
Norway!

All through our lives my sister and I had wanted to visit Europe together, and especially to see Norway, the land where our grandparents were born. In 1998, after our mother had died, we were able to fulfill our life-long dream. June took me to Norway. Christy Lynn gave me a lovely journal for the journey, hoping I would record the joyful experience. On the cover was one of my favorite quotations, "Angels can fly because they take themselves lightly". I kept a running narrative.

In Oslo we visited the Vigeland Sculpture Park and saw what may well be the most magnificent collection of sculpture in the world. We traveled to Bergen by train, and went to Edvard Grieg's summer home, where a presentation in his own words brought the great musician to life for me as a spokesman for freedom and love, a man of the people and a gentle spirit whose philosophy I share.

In Stevanger, we visited the cathedral where our great grandparents, Thorbjorn and Elizabeth, were christened and Saint Petre Church where they were wed October 10, 1866.

They were among the first couples married in the new kirk, which opened August third of that year.

"Good Folk"

As we were walking past a pub near the harbor June noticed a freestanding sign which she thought must translate as, "No folk singers; Good folk drinkers". With a message like that I had to take a picture of the sign. As I was aiming the camera, a young Norwegian man stopped to greet us, ask what we were doing. He had never before seen anyone photograph a sign. We told him what message we thought we were capturing, and he corrected our reading of the sign amid much laughter. It was actually a quotation from Gorman, a writer, playwright, philanthropist and supporter of Norske theatre. "Where good people (folk) serve; good people can drink". Gorman, he told us, was good folk.

Trondhjem street art

Trondhjem is my grandmother's birthplace, and in this thousand-year-old city, I felt I had come home. As everywhere in Norway the people are beautiful inside and out. The Nidaros Cathedral in Trondhjem is at least twice the size of the one in Stevanger, and has an impressive political and religious history. Here kings are crowned! This is high school graduation week, so the city is garlanded with beautiful, funny teens. All are garbed in bright pants or overalls, red or checkered white and black, with peaked caps and white lab coats on which they have drawn all manner of pictures and autographs. Some of the youngsters have water guns, and all are friendly, merry and full of good clean fun! These are a people with a huge sense of humor and fun! There are beautiful sculptures everywhere and even the manhole covers are works of art, with raised impressions of Saint Olav and royal crowns.

At the state archives we found records of Jetta Aalbu's sailing and learned that all the Aalbu family were located in Oppdal, about two hours from Trondhjem. On our last night in Trondhjem we spoke of this to our taxi driver and had a surprise response. He said, "Ya! Oppdal! I have cousins named Aalbu in Oppdal. And I have a cousin named Aalbu in Huntington Beach, California. You are leaving tomorrow. If you could stay, I would take you to my home". He hugged us and wished us all the best. A distant cousin had been found. And aren't we all distant cousins? I feel it here so strongly because the national personality is so like our father's, the merry, mischievous, hospitable nature that is Norway. To have been here with my sister in joy before the cancer took her, I have been truly blessed.

In August of 1999 June died, and I realized I am the last of our Isaksen family, and the matriarch of the remaining clan. No one shares the memories of my childhood, or knows the stories of my growing. This telling will be for the children and their children. And so I wrote of my parents' romantic beginnings and endings:

Cholly and Babe

April 1919— Charles Arthur Isaksen, recently returned from naval duty in Puerto Rico, was flexing his acting muscles in a show put on by the Camp Dix Buddy Boys. The venue was Camden, New Jersey. In the third row of the little auditorium, 16-year-old Lily Clara Lemline sat with her girlfriend Magdelene, anxious for the show to begin. Waiting for the 5-minute call, one of Charlie's fellow actors stole an illicit peek at the audience through the frayed curtain and spotted Lily. "I like that little dark-haired one in the third row", he said, and Charlie took a look. "The hell you say", Charlie countered, "She's mine!" Three months later, July 19, 1919, Lil married this "older man" (aged 23) she called Cholly. He lovingly christened her "Babe". Sixty-six years passed, and the fragile old gentleman lay in a hospital bed, drifting in and out of consciousness after a stroke. Lillian, his wife, asked him, "Cholly, can you see me?" He replied, "Babe, I could see you fifty yards away through a hole in a curtain". And he passed from this life on the sweetness of her kiss.

June had told her sons she wanted me to have her expensive lavender automobile, and we talked about the wisdom of achieving this ownership here across the nation. We decided instead, that Steven would sell the vehicle and send me the money, which paid for a secondhand Ford Contour, some dental work, and joy of joys—hearing aids! I also invested a small sum in becoming certified by the American Academy of Bereavement in June's honor. The "peculiarity of mind" I noted when writing for the weekly newspapers was a skill that made writing memorials flow naturally for me. I was gifted with the ability to "know" the deceased, whom I may have never met, by interviewing the bereaved. Most often the reaction to my services was, "He (or she) would have loved it!" It seemed appropriate that I be recognized as a bereavement counselor. The course of study reinforced what I had already learned in my ministry over the years.

When I went to New Jersey to help my nephews with the aftermath of June's death, I became aware once more of the clutter that invades life when we lose touch with simplicity. June had so much "stuff" and she left notes that were never meant to be read by others. I returned home and gave away about one third of my furniture and various belongings, which were not excessive to begin with. Then I re-read my twelve journals. I had written of so much poverty, struggle and pain—too much sorrow for me to leave those images behind. Personal moments, emotions and expressions of sexuality were not meant to be shared nor to burden those left behind.

Having extracted my best work for publication, I destroyed
the books. Still I honor the writing of my

Journals

A journal...
  once I kept a journal
  filled with the magic of awareness
  the spark of excitement
  the salty drops of my despair.
My senses opened and responded
  and my very sensing
  became more real
  as I recorded
  the fullness of living
  on the waiting page
I am a different woman
  from the writer of that
  early journal
  that record
  of the nascent poet/philosopher
I have lived several lives
  and become a new metaphor.
  My myths have mellowed
  and my symbols changed
I have been sunflower,
  sailboat, wheat
  and flowing stream
  scent of autumn
  or strawberries and musk
I have growing to do
  and miracles to discover
  I am anxious and serene
  desirable and frightening

in my potency
As my senses continue
    to drink in life
    to reach out and touch
    everyone and everything.
    And the poetry of experience
    again fills the page.

I saw Rosie O'Donnell being interviewed on TV about some controversy she'd experienced, and she said, "If I had been braver, I'd just have cried". Braver, perhaps, and wiser. In those days I wrote about in my journals, when life was tougher than even I choose to remember today, I would not let myself cry in front of my daughters. I feared I would upset them, or maybe appear weak and unable to take care of them and protect them. At one of my lowest points, money was almost non-existent and Charlie Reed told me there was a position open up the mountain at deBenneville Pines. I said, "We don't have much, but I couldn't bear to give up what little we have—our home". I wept, there in Brewers card shop, and Charlie just stood there with me and let me cry. He didn't make a big thing of it, but he made me feel accepted and supported. I realized I had been short-changing my daughters. I'd taught them empathy and caring, and I'd held them when they cried. Why should I deny them my own tears? Why not let them be the gentle, caring, supportive and comforting women they had become? I began to share more.

One afternoon I returned from an errand to find a police car in front of my cottage. When I walked out to check, I saw Audrey Peterson sitting on her back step with the policemen. She introduced me to them. They were there because her bi-polar daughter had committed suicide beside our side fence while Audrey was away at an appointment. Her house and property were to be off-limits for a while, so the officers asked if they might use my living room to talk with her, and eventually with her other daughters. I made them welcome. Soon the deputy coroner arrived, and I was greatly impressed with the gentle, orderly manner in which she carried out her work. There was great compassion and kindness shown by both Huntington Beach Police and Orange County Coroners!

May 2, 2000, Amy and Matt presented us with another beautiful baby boy, and named him Jacob Riley. This was surely the live wire of the family and a particular delight to his Aunt Kristi because this time she didn't have any wee ones of her own to enjoy. Jake did not usher in a flood of cousins, but held the position of family dynamo alone.

One of the inside jokes or wise sayings we Somers share came from *A Path With Heart*, by Jack Kornfield, a Buddhist monk and teacher. The idea is that everyone, not just "someone" or one of my community or clan, but everyone I meet in my life, is a Buddha or enlightened one. Everyone, that is, except me or except you. But that's OK. We are the very *raison d'être* for all of these Buddhas, we and our need for enlightenment are why they exist and why they behave as they do. (This seems a slightly solipsist point of view, but bear with me.) We recognize that everyone who crosses our path is there to teach us. Each one does this by acting in whatever way they act, for the sole purpose of bringing insights and needed experiences into our life. They are providing the teachings and the difficulties we need, so that we will "awaken". They are there for our growth and enlightenment. What are the lessons they offer? Does the driver who cuts me off on the freeway perhaps instruct me in patience, in driving more cooperatively and carefully myself, or in compassion, perhaps, as I concern myself with his endangered safety and the safety of others whom he might endanger? Or must the lesson be repeated again and again and again, until I get it right? So whenever any of us meets someone who frustrates us, behaves rudely toward us, or causes us inconvenience, we remind ourselves and one another that this may be our personal Buddha, and we smile.

Chapter twenty
Nearer God's heart in a garden

In my mother's dooryard there was a little sign that read:

> The kiss of the sun for pardon
> The song of the birds for mirth
> One is nearer God's heart in a garden
> Than anywhere else on earth.

This, too, has helped to shape my life.

By the turn of the new century, looking at my growing store of poems and short essays, I decided the time had come for me to publish a second collection. The writing flowed well, and my herb garden inspired a theme, but I hesitated to begin the illustrations, which I planned as pencil drawings. I felt unsure of my ability to produce anything worthwhile. Dragging my feet, I found noble things to do, like cleaning closets or mopping floors. Then I joined a spiritual class at CRS and the drawings almost magically appeared beneath my hand. The book, *Pineapple Sage*, was ready for print within the year.

Shortly after my interim ministry in Mission Viejo had finished, the vendors who put on the weddings on the Royal

Caribbean ships chose to discontinue their affiliation, and that source of income closed to me. The costs of maintaining my home in HB became overwhelming. Around this time Kristi came to HB to talk with her Mom about the breaking up of her marriage to Jean. He would be moving out of their home into a ranch he had bought nearby, where he could easily co-parent their children with her. They agreed the welfare of their children came first and worked out ways to make the little ones feel secure.

When my seventieth birthday approached, Kristi asked if I wanted to celebrate it with a party, and I happily concurred. I was glad to tell the world I had reached this milestone looking and behaving vibrant and alive. Let them look at my life and say, "If that's seventy, I don't mind this thing called aging". Amy put together an album of letters and pictures, which people had sent remembering me, and she gave it to me with a box of tissues, to mop up any happy sentimental tears. As her contribution to the book, Gail celebrated me with a list of "70 Things I Know and Love about Dori", resoundingly honoring me with her love and respect as well as her wit and mischief.

Still celebrating my birthday a few weeks later, Amy and Matt, Kristi and I went to a Rockapella concert at the Galaxy Theatre in Costa Mesa. When Kevin, the lead singer, came into the audience, I reached out to give him a hug, and he took me up on stage. He asked my name and I told him, "Dori". He asked me to spell it and handed me the mike, and in my sexiest low-pitched, radio voice, I announced: D – O – R – I. The audience went wild. The boys sang "Pretty Woman" to me and when I told one of them (Scott) I'd just turned seventy and was accustomed to using a microphone as a minister, he said, "Wow! I want to go to that church!" I received a standing ovation

SNAPSHOTS
Looking
at old photos, I can see
that I have changed so much
and not at all.
Surrounded still
by wild tribes
of the young...
and still laughing!
Life,
with all its drama,
trauma,
stress,
and tears
remains in truth
—to me—
so very sweet.
And I have yet so much
to taste, to learn,
so much I can
discover and explore!

The picture that inspired this poem was taken forty years ago of me seated on the Stafford parsonage steps with at least a dozen youngsters—mine and everyone else's—clustered around me. That photo has long since disintegrated from being loved to death, but there are so many others in my memory and in the memories of the children. From the days of Dori's Dorm in Fullerton I hear from them:

Hi Dori, I was cruising and saw your website. It was great to see your smiling face even through cyber space. I just had to take a minute to tell you that you truly blessed my life. I'm sure I didn't speak that to you when I was a self-absorbed teen. I'm a minister now at a little Disciples of Christ church in Sparks Nevada. Anyway - you are one of those people who profoundly impacted me on my life journey. Thank you for the ministry you provided - I think you were the "Thespian Chaplain" and we didn't even know it. I guess that's the best way to be a pastor.

* *Dori, Thank you for being so willing to let grace, peace and light to shine. I always felt so welcomed, loved and accepted in your presence. I learned a lot from you and didn't have any idea I was learning at the time. Love, Steve*

* *Did you know that we all thought we were your favorite? You did such a great job being our counselor, friend and pastor. Thanks for all the energy and heart you poured out. God gave you such a gift. Thanks for sharing it!*

* *Dori you had my soul at "Hi! I'm Dori..". You have no idea the impact you really made in our lives and love of life besides the fact you have great kids!!!*

In the early spring of my seventieth year, I was invited to preach at South County UU Church in Mission Viejo, and learned that they had been told no interim minister was available to carry them through the next half year. I asked if they would like to see my ministerial "packet" and they said yes. They were delighted with my experience and called me to serve the church for the next five months. I designed a teaching ministry in which I concentrated on community building, celebrations, churchmanship, UU history and identity, generosity and thankfulness. This was the sweetest group of people I'd met in any UU church, willing to explore something new, to re-encounter something that may not have worked before, to celebrate and to accept and to love. They learned to address me the way CRS members address their clergy, by my first name with the honorific "Reverend". We do this to express warmth and friendship along with respect for the calling of ministry. They rejoiced at my aesthetic improvements, and celebrated one another and me.

While commuting to Mission Viejo, I decided to look for a more comfortable piece of furniture for my living room. Because of my increasing arthritis, I wanted a chaise lounge. On an exploring expedition I found a second-hand consignment shop in Aliso Viejo, the community I'd dubbed Stepford because of its high-priced perfection and uniformity. The shop was filled with the rich folk's formerly owned stuff and I spotted a tapestry lounge chair that was one third the price of any others I'd seen. I paid for it and had it held until I could arrange for a friend to transport it to HB. In the meanwhile I drew a picture of my purchase for Justin and told him I'd be giving away my sofa or my reading chair to make room for the chaise. "Oh, DeeDee!" he howled, "not the pink chair!!" and of course it was the sofa that left.

Although my stay in Mission Viejo was a short one, it was rich with affection. People said things like, "She's so nice!" as if that were something special, and I was shocked that "nice" wasn't automatically to be expected of any minister. When I left, the congregation gave me a big farewell party and gifted me with books and money. Rachel Tutusko, a teen-aged girl in the congregation, wrote a poem which was a beautiful insightful image of the bridge-building that comprises an interim ministry, honoring my time with them. It was called

"Since You've Taught Us How To Love" and spoke of the new path I journeyed with them. I was honored and proud.

As time went on, I saw more and more of my dear Gail, even as she moved from place to place herself. She became family in every way but bloodlines and I shared with her my stories and concerns, knowing she was to be depended upon for emotional support, gardening enjoyment and shopper companionship. It delighted me to cook for a loved one once again and we loved sharing a "Tomato Mary" (Gail's name for it) or a G & T and laughing about nearly everything. She constantly surprised me with tales of all I'd taught her.

I had been in pain with my shoulders and hips for several years, and my arthritis was making simple tasks harder and harder. Living so far from family, however, there was no one to help me. Combined physical and economic pressures finally made it impossible for me to remain in my beloved little beach house. In a place where once there was a developing ghetto, the city of La Mirada had sponsored an urban renewal project, and Breezewood Village was born, just a mile and a half from Amy and her family. I put my name on the waiting list for an apartment and I was one of the fortunate first residents in the beautiful complex. This gracious senior housing village has lush landscaping, practical interior layout, and craftsman-style decorative touches that make it a veritable garden and a lovely place to live. The neighborly residents make it even more so.

On the day in August of 2002 when I moved into Breezewood Village, Kristi, Matt and Amy did the heavy work and I did the organizing. The "grands" stayed home at their respective houses. When Justin's parents returned home, he asked immediately, "Where did DeeDee put the pink chair?" They assured him that the reading chair in my apartment and his place on my lap were secure, and so it was for some time to come. Moving from a roomy three bedroom house with a yard and a mini barn into a tidy but minimal one-bedroom apartment meant giving away even more of my furnishings, books, kitchenware and tools. I had to slim down by more than 70%. My belongings continued to trickle away over the next several years, as I found ways to ease the crowding and open up my space. It has been my habit to rearrange my furniture regularly throughout the years, and that has not changed. Only my physical capacity to lug big heavy items from here to there has diminished, often causing my girls to scold me for overdoing.

Arthritis has given me major problems for a long time, and by 2002 the worst effects settled in my right hip. Dr. George sent me to the best man he knew for hip replacement, Dr. Thomas Schmalzried, a surgeon at Orthopedic Hospital in Los Angeles. Kristi went to my appointment with me and we shivered and quaked as we looked at a display of artificial joints that looked like torture instruments on the wall of the office waiting room. "What do you suppose the doctor's like?" she asked me. "Oh, Kristi", I said, "With a name like Schmalzried, he's got to be good!" He was indeed a sweetheart— gentle and kind as well as skilled. I went into the hospital in early January 2003, and both Kristi and Amy were beside my bed making me laugh as I was being prepared for surgery. I carefully arranged my hospital mobcap to look like a fashionable beret. When I came out of post-op and returned to my room I asked the girls, "How's my hat?" and we laughed some more. When Kristi came to take me home to her house for a period of recovery she brought me a little white teddy bear wearing a pink beret. Although Laura had to give up her bedroom for my use during my stay, she proudly told me how glad she was that I was staying with them instead of with their cousins. Now that's heart room!

With my Breezewood home so close to the Budds family I was able to pick up Justin from Meadow Green School after classes and bring him home with me to do his homework. When he was done he would just visit, play "Where in the World is Carmine San Diego?" or watch a video with me. His favorite video was *Les Miserables*. Sometimes Madeline came to DeeDee's to do her homework as well. Vegas continued to welcome guests, and became a bit less snobbish with the humans in her neighborhood. Everyone in Breezewood soon knew her, and if she slipped past me and out the front door a neighbor would bring her home. I showed Maddie something I called my "doggie dance" which was a little twirl to untangle myself from Vegas's leash, and she taught it to Jake with an extra bump and grind.

At the time of Amy's wedding, I made the mistake of projecting my own attitudes onto my daughter, June. I knew if my sister were having a big wedding, I'd want to be there, no matter what. I thought back to my disappointment at being left out of my parents' sixtieth wedding anniversary, and I assumed Junie would feel the same kind of pain I'd felt, if left out of this celebration. So I scrimped and saved and put together the money to fly her here from Maine for the wedding. Since all the bridal attendants' gowns were being handmade for them here, there would be no opportunity to fit June, so she was not asked to be a bridesmaid. Nor was Ken included in the invitation to attend, because there was not enough money to bring him here. June came to California reluctantly, though she didn't tell me she preferred not to come. She missed Ken desperately, and felt left out because she wasn't a bridesmaid. Her disappointment darkened her days while she was here, making me and everyone else sadly uncomfortable. I regretted my mistake, and worried about being a bad parent.

In 1998 June and Ken were married in Bangor in a civil ceremony, and chose not to tell us until after the fact. This saddened me, too, because we would have liked to be thinking of them at the time of their marriage, to bless them with our love even at this distance, and to send gifts and good wishes. It's easy to blame myself for sad events in my children's lives, but I know that's not fair, nor accurate. We are the products of the choices we have made day by day throughout our lives, so I can also look at our happy choices and rejoice. Little things can make a big difference. This autobiography is not an exposé, scandal sheet, or true confession, but a remembering of the lessons taught by the events that have shaped me, and the people who have made my life so interesting.

From Ann Grogan with her monthly trips to the seashore, from my mother's lovely fingernails tinted Windsor Rose, from psych workshops I've attended, I've learned about self-care. When I lived in Encino, I invested in myself and began going to a nail salon for monthly manicures. And with little to spend on my wardrobe, I have often chosen to make the most of my outfits with scarves or earrings or silk flowers. Kristi's brother-in-law dubbed me "Rosie" because of this style consciousness of mine, and Kristi named my bedroom "Accessory Heaven". Elias, at age 12 told me, "DeeDee, you have such a flare", and the grands even know which colors are DeeDee's colors. Somewhere along the way, I decided my color coordination, grooming, hairstyle and manicure were not for any public, whoever that might be. They were for me, the woman in the mirror. She must matter. I knew it was important to put on lipstick and a lovely colorful tunic even though no one but that woman in the mirror would ever see it. Perhaps this was even more true because I never thought of myself as a beauty or a man-magnet. I was just an ordinary woman living this extraordinary life.

Still there were men who loved me—often younger than I. And nobody had come up with that interesting term, "Cougar", for women like Mary Tyler Moore or me—women who are not defined by the number of our years, but by the vitality of our living. As I look back, even some of the men who were my colleagues and contemporaries were a few unnoticeable years younger than my chronological age, but who knew? I'm now a grandmother. That has never fazed me because, as even my great grandnephews will tell you, I continue to think like a teenager—albeit a very smart one. I happily claim my status as DeeDee, the "bestamor", the "tayta", the grandmother. Inspired by the fortieth birthday of a daughter I wrote:

At forty plus . . .

+ I can claim my greatness.
  Marianne Williamson said it and Nelson Mandella repeated it:
  We ask ourselves, who am I to be brilliant, gorgeous, talented and fabulous? Actually, who are you not to be? You are a child of God; your playing small doesn't serve the world".

+ I can accept my own beauty
  Late bloomers and self-deprecators take note.
  The greatest facelift is a smile that starts in the heart.

Wrinkles are just the pleats and tucks
that give your softness style.

+ I can laugh at me
I'm one of God's Jesters.
My "oops" events make great stories,
and if they'll be funny in a year,
I'll let them be funny now!

+ I can indulge my love of the beautiful.
Bathe your eyes in beauty.
Offer beauty to all your senses.
It will create within you an inner beauty
that expresses itself in nobility, gentleness and
courage".
Remember Renoir painted in spite of his agony from
arthritis telling his friend, Matisse, "The pain passes;
the beauty remains".

+ I can use aging eyesight to discover
Streetlight angels and blurred edges that show
how connected everything and everyone is.
Close up is cozy!

+ I can express my creativity
Every time I look through new eyes,
Every time I step outside the pattern,
Every time I dare
I create something worthwhile.
Allowing myself the simple pleasures of reading,
writing,
gardening or creating a new dish instead of being
driven to fill my time with "shoulds and musts" can
also be creative.
So my kitchen floor needs mopping today,

So what Lady. . . God loves you even with dishes in
the sink!

♦ I can learn—In fact I have learned:
If I am fully in the now, I cannot worry myself about
what may be in the future or might have been in the
past.
I need not accommodate anxiety!
Animal companions are not pets to be owned
but friends to be treasured
The children are God made visible to remind
me that everything I see or cannot see is Sacred.
And being forty or fifty or eighty
is just what we choose to make it;
so we'll age with grace and humor,
be wise beyond our years
and stay—at heart—forever young.

Maine has long been a center of poverty in the nation and
in 2004 June called from Bangor to say things had become
financially desperate for her and Ken. Both of them were out
of work and they could no longer keep a roof over their heads.
Ken could bunk in his parents' place while hunting for a job,
but to survive June needed to come home to California. Kristi
arranged to fly her home and Amy, who was working in the
Entertainment Insurance industry, employed her as a nanny
for the three Budds children.

On weeknights June slept at the Budds house, and on
weekends she came to me and slept on an air mattress in my
living room. We enjoyed our time together immensely, with
June always willing to chat, to enjoy Mom's cooking, to share
a glass of sherry, and to laugh. She went with me wherever I
went, grocery shopping, running errands, doing laundry or

whatever. She missed Ken terribly and called him regularly, keeping in sight always the time when she would be able to return to her beloved husband. Sadly, her crabby disposition on weekdays did nothing to endear her to her young charges, but she and I took advantage of the time she was here to bond, as we had never managed to do before. I'd asked her in a phone conversation the year before if I should try to arrange a visit to her in Bangor, and she'd said I shouldn't. Of course I was sure I must have failed her badly and this seeming rejection must be because I hadn't been a good enough mother to her. Now, however, she explained that she would have loved to have me visit, but their lease forbad them from having overnight guests. It never occurred to her that I might stay in a motel and visit with her in the daytime. At last Ken found work and a tiny third floor apartment for them in Augusta, and joyfully, she was able to go home. Once more she became the sender of birthday cards and thank you notes.

While talking with a Breezewood neighbor in the laundry room, I learned she was a member of the Friends of the La Mirada Theatre for the Performing Arts, and I decided that might be just the thing for me. I attended a meeting of the organization, and learned the Friends are the volunteer ushers at the beautiful Broadway style playhouse in my city. I had loved my association with the Friends of the Library in Huntington Beach, so I joined the group, and came to know and appreciate the many friendly volunteers and to enjoy lots of top quality theatre. During my second year in the Friends I was asked to serve as Secretary of the organization for two years. Then I served as President for two years and finally as Parliamentarian for two more. Progressing arthritis prevented me from ushering any longer.

July 16, 2005 Amy and Matt had their fourth child, a beautiful little boy named Austin Michael.

Mark called before the winter holidays to tell me he and Christy Lynn had been in counseling for the past year, and had decided to seek a divorce. He found an apartment near their house, with room for the children to stay part-time with him; the big holidays they all would spend together. I'm thankful for the civilized way in which my children have chosen to handle their most difficult situations.

As 2006 dawned I met with a lovely couple to plan their wedding. I had written their ceremony and when the day approached, I drove to a rehearsal at the home where the wedding was to take place. As I was leaving I crossed the driveway and the uneven surface caught my foot and down I went. I fell on the sidewalk and landed against my left shoulder. When the folks picked me up, my arm was behaving strangely, and I knew it must be broken. The bride's brother drove me home and Amy took me to an after-hours clinic for an x-ray. The break was just below the shoulder joint. Much to my distress, Amy insisted I find a replacement minister to officiate at the wedding the next day. The Rev. Peggy Price filled in for me, using my script and projecting her own sweetness, and the family loved her. Dr. Gerald Swanson, a highly respected sports medicine guru and orthopedic surgeon in Fullerton scheduled me for a total shoulder replacement in May, and once more my girls kept me laughing until I entered the operating room and I emerged with a bionic shoulder.

Baby Austin was treated for clubfeet and then for cataracts, and he seemed to have great difficulty lifting his head. I suspected he might be autistic. I asked Matt what they had learned about the baby's condition, and he assured me Austin was coming along pretty well, but he himself was discontented with police work and with being tied down in marriage. Eventually the doctors discovered that our little angel has cerebral disgenesis and was having epileptic seizures, so Amy and Matt began the endless round of doctors and county support agencies that are necessary to the care of a special needs child. And Amy discovered she had some "special needs" of her own.

In August of 2007 I wrote to my dear friend Marj Wyckoff:

> When Amy was pregnant with Jacob seven years ago, she had an auto accident that actually broke her back. Because of her pregnancy they didn't X-ray, so didn't know about the break. Finally, this spring the pain was totally incapacitating and they discovered the problem. In May they operated—used cadaver bone to fashion two new discs—and she is steadily improving. Her courage, spiritual strength and wit are awe-inspiring. She is my hero. My other news is not happy. June is in Maine Medical Center with fourth stage cancer. She has lost so much weight, down to less than a hundred pounds, and she was a good sized woman. Doctor speaks of months, not years. Her choice is quality of life over quantity, and her husband agrees. Thankfully they have no children. Kristi arranged for me to fly out last week, and my short visit made a big difference to June's spirits. The siblings are scheduled to go next Monday

My comfort is in knowing June was truly happy with her soul-mate, Ken. They played together, creating songs and stories, playacting along with their little collection of videos of Broadway Musicals, and finding simple pleasures to share. Her illness was swift and cruel, and she faced death with courage beyond imagination. When I sat beside her bed she still lit the room with her smile. I spoke with my firstborn on the phone for the last time, and though she couldn't answer, they tell me she relaxed at hearing my voice, and I sent her on the wings of my love to her next adventure. September 18, 2007 she passed from this life peacefully and surrounded by love. Ken's sweet mother called Kristi, and asked her to give me the news. The cosmos was gentle with me, because Gail came to me at once, and we lit candles throughout the apartment and held each other and wept. When I speak of "my girls" Gail is surely one of them.

I dealt with my grief by writing:

> To live the life of June Somers-Cook was to give unconditional love and loyalty, to be quietly forgiving; to laugh joyously whenever a laugh was to be shared, especially with the siblings or her beloved Ken, always appreciating another's wit and talent. It was looking at the world through great blue eyes full of childlike innocence and finding pleasure in simple things— play-reading and play-acting, lifting her sweet voice in song with a chorus or choir, hiking in a bird sanctuary, capturing a snapshot of a lighthouse, playing board games, hanging a new magnet on the refrigerator door, cuddling a huge teddy bear or plush dog, coming up with answers for Jeopardy or watching TV-Land and reruns of M*A*S*H*, and especially just being with her soul-mate, Ken. And remembering... oh, yes you could count on it, Junie always remembered. In any conversation she was sure to say, "I remember..". She remembered names and places,

funny little events, TV episodes, song lyrics, punch lines, anniversaries and birthdays. Nobody was as good as June at remembering birthdays—getting the perfect card for you and magically on time, even from her hospital bed. Life for June was taking delight in that curious tilting of a dog's head, the beauty of flowers and music and the fun of the "Peanuts" gang. It was loving her nieces and nephews and everybody's children, enjoying a luscious burger or a little glass of wine, and giggling over the funny side of just about anything. The human experience, for June, meant brightening everyone's day with her smile, the smile that lit the room!

She had told her sister she wanted to be cremated and to have her memorial service in California. Ken agreed. Kristi found a beautiful little family-owned memorial park in Chatsworth, and there her ashes rest. The marker, with the musical notes of the song There will never be another you reads: "Forever a smile in her heart".

The Budds family had outgrown their house on Ocean Ave. and they moved into a roomy house with a pool on Amy Street in Upland, too far away for me. The neighborhood is beautiful and the schools just right for the kids. A good move for them! But, that summer Matt took Justin, Maddie and Jake with him on a Mexican vacation with his mother's family, leaving Amy at home with Austin. This seemed to me clearly an unloving thing to do and it signaled the dissolution of their marriage. By Christmas he was ready to move out of the house.

As expected, my second hip demanded replacement in 2008. I had been experiencing considerable pain in my left arm, not unlike the pain I'd had when I broke my shoulder, and I was scheduled for hip surgery. Dr. Swanson had X-rays, then special scans of my arm taken, and on the morning of my planned surgery discovered I had a stress fracture in my arm. Did I want to go ahead with the surgery? I said, "Yes!" After the operation, when the in-house physician told me I would have to go to rehab instead of going home with Kristi, I said no. "But you can't use a walker with that broken arm", he said. So that afternoon when he next saw me, I was limping down the hall using a cane instead of a walker. I went home with Kristi.

I have found that the way I feel about things is affected by the way I tell the story. And sometimes the telling is affected by the lessons I have finally learned. A poem written when I was feeling defeated and in the depths rewrote itself several years later, when I was preparing my first book for publication, turning the original sad outcome into a ray of hope. A pivotal line righted itself from: "Ghosts, without you I should die", to "Ghosts, it's time to say goodbye". My story had changed, my message had changed, and so had I.

A colleague, who later came to love me like a little sister, first assumed I was phony and shallow; he was annoyed by what he called my perpetual smile and my sunny greeting. When he learned the smile was genuine, and based on my choosing: "whatsoever things are good, whatsoever things are true, whatsoever things are beautiful, (to) think on these things", he accepted it, got to know me, and learned I was a real person. I, too, had known pain, but I chose to look for the unexpected gifts or lesson the pain and darkness brought. That takes a while sometimes; it takes imagination, and courage. My ministry has been described by several insightful laymen as a ministry of the positive. Just today in the social networking age of "Facebook" I received a message from a former parishioner: "I need not ask if all is well with you because you ALWAYS see the positive in life so all IS well".

Welcome home!

A few years ago I found a fill-in-the-blank book designed to be completed for one's grandchildren, which includes, along with the usual family trees and childhood stories, an array of thoughtful and provocative catalysts beginning My deepest values are... Here are my entries:

* *My deepest values are* Kindness and family, humor, beauty, and creativity.
* *I was proud of* being part of many children's growing and being Mom to four such good people.

- *Everyone thought I shouldn't but I'm glad* I married Irving Stevens, because he gave me Amy and the ministry.
- *A matter of concern was* living up to my values and making a gracious and welcoming home.
- *I was always sorry I* didn't leave the bank job and write for Greater Philadelphia Magazine.
- *I feel very strongly about* the absolute unacceptability of any form of violence; the need for kindness, civility, humor and acceptance.
- *I've changed my mind, and now I think* there are more paths to "the good" than those restricted to Christianity. The cosmos is inclusive, and as a Universalist I know "Everyone is welcome at Creation's table".

There was also a section marked "Your grandfather would want you to know…" I felt inadequate to answer for my former husbands, but I knew what my father had taught me, so I chose to record what Papa Isaksen might have wanted my grandchildren to know. Papa created beauty with his handicrafts and in his garden, and he sought beauty in song and story. I told the children: He would want you to know how to grow wildflowers and how to dance, and that you should never choke a hammer. Papa would teach you, by the way he lived, that anger is wasted energy; that kindness and a warm smile buy happiness; that beauty is a worthy goal.

Most of the grands are teens, now, and the first three are old enough to drive. They make life exciting, each in their own special way, and I am still writing. With the loss of my daughter, and six months later the loss of my companion, Vegas, I self-medicated using literary therapy, which is to say I returned to writing poetry. Amazingly, the poems are not sad, but joyful and full of hope. A favorite piece of wisdom says, "Life isn't about waiting for the storm to pass, it's about learning to dance in the rain". And so I wrote:

Dancing in the Rain
T'would be so easy to give up on life
To rant and rage against the dark
And yet there is a gentle side to life
That whispers hope… and lights a spark.
The fire ignited warms the soul of me.
The image in my mind is clear…
A campfire with the family gathered round,
And friends—with laughter shared and tears.
Life's tragedies bring lessons learned,
Not always welcomed, rarely sought.
Yet in the eyes of loved ones shines
The tender gift the "dark" has brought.
Our common journey, on a stormy path
Each hoping to transcend life's pain,
Will need a dream, an inner truth,
That sets us dancing in the rain.

Self-identified intellectuals in some of the churches I served would have preferred angry or pedantic preaching, and were unmoved by my positive message of love and kindness in an unkind world. When I was guest speaking at another church however, I a distinguished gentleman in the congregation told me, "When I saw this curly haired little woman in a long dress, I thought we were going to hear something frivolous. But you have given me something serious to think about". Why not think seriously about life's positives? Why require wordy academic lectures? It is simply not my style to pontificate. For me authority and wisdom are expressed in poems rather than polemics, stories rather than statutes, discoveries rather than decrees. My deepest understandings sometimes refuse to reveal themselves in ordinary prose. They demand melody, rhythm, meter, and joy. My best thoughts strive to be shortened, condensed, transmuted into poetry.

And so it is.

Immediacy of Poetry

Here…
Now…
    intensified in words
    that carry joy
or pain
or yearning
    fragrances and
    pictures for the mind
    stories lived and told
    in metered rhyme
Now…
Here…
    the poet breathes and wonders
    what is true
    old wisdom clarifies
    and shines anew
    for love
    or learning